Where the Magic Happens!

THE SCIENCE & STORIES BEHIND CHALLENGING YOUR COMFORT ZONE

KEVIN CORCORAN JR.

TRADECRAFT

Tradecraft Books, Los Angeles 90046
Printed in the United States of America
ISBN: 9780998169354
Corcoran Jr., Kevin.
Where the Magic Happens!
The Science & Stories Behind
Challenging Your Comfort Zone
Book cover and interior design: Kevin Corcoran Jr.
Author photo: JonKillz Photography

This book is dedicated to the Captain.

For turning mini-moments into magical memories, and for always being the coolest thing he could be, which was himself.

…and for introducing me to cheesesteaks and red oak.

I love you, Pops.

Contents

"Extraordinary things are always hiding in places people never think to look."

— Jodi Picoult

Introduction

My heart was beating right out of my chest. The room was silent. The lights above the stage were burning as they illuminated a tiny red, circle carpet. I was behind the scenes, doing pushups and jumping jacks, trying to calm myself down. Everyone could feel the energy in the room, like a whirring generator of excitement, curiosity, and passion. Time was frozen as nearly 400 people were waiting for me. For them, it was only a few seconds before I'd take the stage. For me, it was a moment I had been waiting for all my life. This wasn't any old stage. This was TED. … "Please give a warm welcome to our next speaker!"

The very first time I tried to speak publically, I panicked, ran off the stage, cried, then vomited. It was in second grade during a play about dinosaurs. Little did I know, this would be the start of some magic in my life. Years later, I tried again. I went on stage with a rock band that I was in, and I spent the entire time playing wrong notes and hiding behind giant speakers. The band kicked me out. Years later, not much changed. I presented on behalf of Apple at San Diego State University, and I sped through my material, forgot to use my slides, then ended just after three minutes when it was supposed to be a 15 to 20-minute presentation. Public speaking and I were not very good friends. In fact, we didn't really get along at all.

So how in the world did I, a timid introvert with extreme stage-fright, become a public-speaking teacher, a communication specialist, a nationally recognized presenter, and a TEDx speaker? The answer is simple: With a little bit of magic. But not your ordinary kind with rabbits, decks of cards, long ribbons, or handsaws; this is a much different type. Magic is happening all around us, every single day. But most of the time, we miss it. That's because we spend so much time chasing comfort, clinging to old habits, and holding on to what feels familiar.

I once had a teacher who started class by drawing two circles of different sizes on the chalkboard. In the smaller circle, he wrote "Comfort Zone," and in the larger circle he wrote "Where the Magic Happens!" It looked something like this:

This has proven to be one of the most valuable lessons I have ever learned. And it's this idea that serves as the foundation for this book. I've spent the last several years of my life traveling all over the world, meeting with neuroscientists and famous CEOs, working closely with companies like Apple, Sony, and the American Red Cross, and I even met the love of my life in the process. I started to find comfort in the most unusual places. I got lost in the woods in France, met the Buddha in a dusty old dojo, swam in freezing cold Icelandic water, played piano for a big crowd in San Jose, and even rappelled off a 50-foot ledge, in the middle of a storm, in the Eastern Mountains of California. It was these unusual places where I felt charged up in a way I never had before. It was like I hooked my life up to a pair of jumper cables and revved the engine. The best part? Anyone can do what I did and learn what I learned.

Not only is challenging your comfort zone helpful for public speaking, but it can also help with getting jobs, negotiating salaries, achieving promotions, meeting new friends, building new relationships, earning more money, having more fun, and doing what was previously thought to be impossible. In the following pages, I will be sharing my own wild stories about stepping outside my comfort zone, explaining the science of why it was beneficial, and finally, offering themed comfort challenges for you to be a part of the action. Let the *magic* begin!

1

The Rescue

I couldn't believe my eyes. The place was a bloodbath – an absolute massacre. My ears faded in and out between screams of people in horrific pain and frantic terror. The weather was incredibly stormy, the kind of rain that makes it hard to keep your eyes open. We were lost, somewhere out in the wilderness, and help was too far away. This was something we had to handle on our own.

The amount of bad luck and complete misfortune that happened in a matter of seconds was unbelievable. Someone had been struck by lightning and fell off a two-story cliff. Another person had been stung by a swarm of bees, and he was allergic. Someone else had been climbing, slipped, then fell backward and cracked his head on the rocky floor. One woman stopped breathing altogether and collapsed to the ground. There was a young man who nearly had his arm severed by an oversized tree branch that fell on him. A middle-aged woman was having a full-blown panic attack and running around shouting uncontrollably. There were only five of us who were still in good enough condition to help the others. I looked to my friend, and I could see the flicker of fear in her eyes. I shifted my focus to the other 'rescuers' on my team. That same flicker was in all of their eyes. All I could think was: "Thank God none of this was real."

*   *   *

Driving down a narrow highway out in the backcountry of Southern California, it was early in the morning, and I was amped for my next adventure. I had one of my favorite songs playing, *Back to the Earth*, by Jason Mraz, the windows were partially cracked for some cool, fresh air, and the sun was doing an early morning dance on my dashboard. On the outside, I felt great. I cherished my job as a teacher, I had a girlfriend whom I loved, and I had a tribe of friends that would do anything for me.

On the inside, however, I was scared out of my mind. I was on my way to a Wilderness First Responder training, which is a course designed to teach advanced medical skills in the wild. I recently decided that I wanted to become a Mountain Rescue Team member and possibly start my own adventure business down the road, so this training was mandatory. For someone who was scared of blood, fearful of getting injured, not very good at taking the lead, and secretly not very confident, this course sure seemed like a bad idea, which is exactly why I knew it would be good for me.

The training was held in a remote cabin, way out in the eastern backcountry of San Diego. There was no cell phone reception, no giant grocery stores, no freeways, and definitely no easy way out. In other words, quitting would take more effort than sticking it out. I parked my car in the dirt lot and walked inside the cabin. Sprawled out on the floor was a body with blood all over. I nearly vomited on the spot. Next to it, there were syringes, bandages, rotting pig legs, sleeping bags, an amputated arm, and a make-shift stretcher. The whiteboard on the front wall had just a couple words written, "Get ready." I gulped, just like a cartoon character, and sat down in a chair at the very back of the room.

As our instructor, a slender man with sunburnt orange hair, a pair of tactical pants, and extra-large, mountainous boots, approached the front of the room, he began his introduction. He announced his name was Wyatt, and that he had spent the last 11 years working as a firefighter, an EMT, and a wilderness rescuer. "I've seen more than any man should have to see. You name it, amputated legs, fractures with the bones sticking out, waterfalls of blood, and my least favorite, animal attacks. Where there is adventure, there is always danger on the other side of it. This course just might save your life one day." I bit my cheek and shifted nervously in my seat.

Once he was finished introducing himself, he asked for a volunteer to go next. I looked down at my desk to avoid eye contact. A stocky man with muscles bulging out of his shirt stood up, stroked his grizzly beard, and proudly said, "My name is Jeff and I'm a wildland firefighter. Remember those crazy wildfires back in 08'? Well, I was there. In fact, I almost didn't make it out alive. So, I'm thankful to be here because I need to brush up on my medical skills, especially since I use them every day." Everyone clapped and welcomed him, and I immediately felt like I was out of place. As the introductions continued, there was an Alaskan explorer, a professional backpacker, a Canadian version of Bear Grylls, an Arizona river guide, a prison camp counselor, and a guy who made over six figures but chose to live in a van. Oh, and then there was me, a nerdy communication teacher who lacked real confidence and couldn't stand to see people get hurt.

After introductions, Wyatt asked us to mingle with each other while he stepped outside to grab some of the course content. Specifically, he told us to "get comfortable with everyone because we'd be saving lives together." I laughed to myself, thinking, "That's one way to kick off a week with new people." I looked around at my soon-to-be friends, some were sipping on coffee, others were waiting for their tea to cool. Almost every single person in the room had a double-wall, vacuum insulated canteen of some kind. Most were scratched, dented, and had stickers from national parks, campgrounds, and other adventures they had been on in the past. When I looked down at my own hands and saw a flimsy, plastic cup that came free as part of a bagel special near my house, I, again, felt very out of place.

Just then, Wyatt ran into the room with wide eyes and a shrill voice. He shouted, "You guys! There's been an accident. Cindy twisted her ankle, collapsed to the ground, and broke some ribs. I was able to get her into the stretcher, but it's up to you to secure the litter so that we can get her out of here safely."

I spilled some of the hot, minty tea from the plastic cup on my hands as I was quickly putting it down, which burned like minty hell. But, before I could whine about it, I saw the other students had already run out the door, so I raced after. We hurried outside to Cindy and saw that she was in pretty bad shape. She had wounds all over her legs, her body was twisted, and her face was scrunched up with pain. We worked together to wrap straps around the stretcher she was in, while one of the rescue students consoled her, "Cindy, everything is going to be okay." People started fumbling with the ropes and straps. I didn't tell anyone this, but the only knot I ever learned was for tying shoes. I watched as several of them twisted their hands and finagled some truly spectacular rope work. Wyatt called out to me, "You're not doing much good just standing there. Help your team secure the litter." Nodding my head, I knelt down and picked up some rope. I figured if I just made it look like I was doing something, I'd go unnoticed. Then, one of the other students said to me, "Tie that rope off right there, that'll keep her bottom half secure." Nervous as hell, I slipped the rope under the stretcher, brought it over the top, and tied several shoelace style knots. I just kept tying the same knot over and over, thinking that if I did it enough times it would be secure.

After about 10 minutes, we had what we thought was a rock-solid wrap job. Except, of course, for the knot that I had tied. I was a little worried about that. Cindy was moaning and the wounds on her legs looked terribly painful. We were instructed to lift the stretcher as a team of six people. Quickly, we decided who would be hands-on and who would be off to the side. I tried to persuade my way out. The thought of being watched by everyone else, while doing something I had no idea how to do, scared the hell out of me. I found myself in the most unusual place. On one hand, I wanted to learn these skills so that I could be a rescue-team member and adventure-business owner, but on the other, I was paralyzed with the fear of failure, of being judged by my fellow rescuers, and of not being good enough to be a part of the team.

Before I knew what was happening, I found myself in the middle, between people who backed away and people who grabbed hold of the stretcher. They needed one more pair of hands, and the clock was ticking. I tried to take a step back, but just as I did, Jeff yelled, "Come on Kev. We need one more." Damn!

I bent down and grabbed hold of the cold, steel rail that lined the side of the stretcher. Closing my eyes, I tried to imagine that I was anywhere else. "Alright boys," Jeff said, "On the count of three we'll lift her up. Nice and easy." I looked around to the others and felt envious of their confidence. "One…" I tightened my grip. "Two…" I clenched my teeth. Maybe they couldn't see it on my face, but I was ready to piss my pants. "Three!" Cindy yelled with fear as we hoisted her up. The stretcher rocked and swayed, like the turbulence of a plane tumbling through a storm. "Alright, good, now level her out," Jeff yelled. How was he so damn confident?

Now that Cindy was suspended in midair, Wyatt spoke up, "Good enough so far. Now turn the litter upside down." One of our team members laughed, thinking it was a joke. Wyatt stared at him and took a step closer. "I'm not kidding," he said. One of the students snapped back, "Wait a second, what if Cindy falls out?" "Then you better hope you've done a good enough job. You're here to rescue her after all." The Canadian version of Bear Grylls was amped, "Let's just go for it. I think it's good enough." "What do you mean you think it's *good enough*?" Cindy yelled from the stretcher.

"Whatever, here we go on the count of three." After his count, we slowly started rotating the stretcher. When it was completely upside down, I panicked. If the knot I tied came undone, Cindy could fall flat on her face and get even more injured. I kept telling myself that everything would be okay. I looked over to the bottom half of the carrier and noticed one of the ropes slowly slipping. We kept rotating. I didn't know whether to speak up about the loosening rope or keep quiet. Cindy called out from underneath, "You guys, I think it's getting loose down by my waist." "Don't worry Cindy," Jeff's voice boomed, "We're experts. We used butterfly knots, clove hitches, and bowlines so there's no way this thing is coming undone." I kept quiet. My shoelace-style knot did not qualify as any of those. The stretcher suddenly felt very heavy. I prayed that it would hold. And as luck would have it, the rope held... for a few seconds.

Just then, the rope snapped back and whipped around like a snake attacking its prey. Cindy screamed. We nearly dropped her as some of us lost our footing. The stretcher rocked like a small boat in a big storm. Back and forth, up and down, it bobbed and dipped. One of her legs dangled out from the straps and she screamed louder. All of us were shuffling our feet and adjusting to the different weight. I was freaking out, but everyone else seemed to maintain their composure. "Easy does it," Jeff yelled, "We've got this." We quickly rotated her back upright, then slowly lowered her to the floor. I let out a huge, thankful sigh. Wyatt looked upset, "Cindy would be dead if this was a real rescue. When extracting a patient from the wilderness, the stretcher has to be secure enough to be taken out by a helicopter. If she was heli-vac'd right now, she'd fall right out and die a miserable death. So, good thing this isn't real. Now, re-wrap the stretcher, get her over that tree, and under that truck." A couple students giggled.

"Damn it, I'm not kidding. Cindy is dying. Save her or you fail."

I wish I could say that we magically got her to safety in the next few minutes, but it took us a whopping four hours to get her to the extraction point. No breaks, no water, no food. Just lifting, carrying, and maneuvering. He wasn't kidding. We actually had to lift the stretcher over a wide tree trunk and lower it underneath a small pickup truck. We may have banged Cindy's head a couple times while trying to shove her under the truck, but thank God Wyatt had his back turned.

The week went on and the lessons got wilder. We were taught over 24 hours of lectures, assigned over 300 pages of readings, and practiced all different types of scenarios. Slowly, I was starting to get the hang of things. With each new lesson and mission, I was getting slightly more confident because there was no other option. I couldn't quit, I couldn't run away, I couldn't resist and still pass, so I kept my focus on finding comfort in the chaos. Even when we gave epinephrine shots to each other, treated hypothermia, used rotten pigs' legs to learn how to clean wounds, and rescued someone who was run over by a car, I kept searching for a sense of comfort in all of the choreographed craziness.

After a couple more cabin lessons and outdoor scenarios, it was time for a late lunch on our last day. Sitting at a picnic table with some of my new friends, I treated myself to a smooshed PB&J and an apple. All of a sudden, while I was about halfway through the sandwich, Wyatt ran over, waving his arms and shouting, "Get up, there's been an accident! And this one is real!" I watched as a few other responder students ran out of the cabin with their trail packs and first aid kits. Shocked, I dropped the PB&J, darted into the cabin, grabbed my backpack, and hurried out to follow the others. As we ran, I looked around and noticed there were only five of us. Where was everyone else?

We rounded the dirt road, careened into a canyon, hacked our way through some overgrown bushes, and stumbled into a massacre. All I could hear was screaming. Everywhere I looked was a death trap. One student had been struck by lightning. Another student had been stung by a swarm of bees. Someone else cracked his head on the rocky floor. One woman collapsed to the ground and wasn't breathing. There was a young man who nearly had his arm severed. There were only five of us who were in good enough condition to help the others. I looked to my friend, and I could see the flicker of fear in her eyes. I shifted my focus to the other 'rescuers' on my team. That same flicker was in all of their eyes. And above all the noise and carnage, Wyatt shouted, "Kevin, you're in charge."

My heart sank. My knees felt like they were going to buckle. Panic set in, and I could feel nervousness flood through my entire body. I had come a long way over the past week, but I didn't feel ready for this. My heart banged like the beat of a war drum. My palms leaked with flooding sweat. My head spun in fast motion. For a moment, I paused and truly thought about the past week. I thought about Jeff and his inspiring leadership. I thought about Wyatt and his powerful stories. I thought about myself, and how making it to this point was something worth celebrating. For someone who was scared of blood, fearful of getting injured, not very good at taking the lead, and secretly not very confident, this week had changed everything. I wanted to quit several times and walk away from the discomfort. I wanted to give up and leave the challenge behind. I wanted to forfeit and surrender to the defeat.

But, I realized this was an opportunity to step up to the challenge. This past week I had gained more than just training; I gained a newfound sense of confidence and belief in myself. So, in that moment, I chose to rise up like a warrior.

"Alright team, get ready! This is what we've been trained to do," my voice boomed through the storm and the screams. I pointed toward the nearby hill and shouted, "Alexis, you head up to the top of that hill and be on lookout." Alexis nodded her head and darted off toward the hill. "Tony, I need you to find us the safest extraction route. If there are branches, roots, or bushes in the way, hack them down and make it possible." Tony nodded his head. He set down his backpack, pulled out a mini machete, held it up in the air, and let out a victory cry as he ran off in the other direction. "For the rest of us, let's split up and stabilize. Try to find whoever is in the worst shape and help them first." We huddled together and let out a battle cry, "Let's go!"

The daylight was fading behind the darkness of the clouds. On top of the thunderous storm, the approaching blackness of night was making the rescue even more difficult. I dug through my backpack to find my headlight, strapped it on tight, clicked the switch, and scanned the scene. The heavy rainfall made the ground incredibly slippery. I could feel my boots digging deeper into the mud as I stood still. Every few seconds, thunder cracked and lightning fired. I tried to wipe some of the sweat, rain, and dirt off my face; I could feel it smear as my hand dragged. Bodies were everywhere. I squinted my eyes, clenched my teeth, and sprinted toward the lightning strike victim.

As I approached, I chucked my backpack off and knelt down beside the man who had been struck by lightning. "Sir, my name is Kevin and I'm a Wilderness First Responder, I'm here to help." He looked straight into my eyes and let out the most horrific, blood-curdling squeal. When looking at his body, there was more blood visible than skin. His clothing was burned and ripped all over. I looked up to the rock-face that was next to us, back down at him, back up to the cliff, and realized he must have been climbing when he was struck, then fallen about two stories or so. "Can you hear me?" He didn't respond. He just kept violently shaking. Suddenly, my walkie-talkie crackled and a garbled voice came on, "We have six patients, all in pretty bad shape. Most important right now are the lightning strike, the allergic bee sting, the cracked head, and the severed arm. Over." I clicked the button and responded, "Thanks Alexis. Copy that. I'm with the lightning strike patient. Jeff, you'll take the person who hit their head, Dale, you'll take the severed arm, and Bear, you'll take the bee sting victim. Over and out."

The next two hours were some of the craziest of my life. The rain seemed to fall harder and the storm seemed to get worse, which made the rescue much more intense. I ran from patient to patient, treated severe wounds, stabilized injuries, and continued to oversee my entire team. I was pouring sweat and loving every second of it.

As we gathered to celebrate our successful rescue, there were cheers and high-fives. Even Wyatt was smiling at this point. I looked around at my team, at the beautiful chemistry of recent strangers coming together to do the impossible, and I felt the most unbelievable sense of awe. Sure, the lightning was flashing, the thunder was cracking, the rain was heavy, and we were in the middle of nowhere. But, comfort can always be found in the most unusual places. And that, of course, is where the magic happens.

The Science Behind
Comfort Challenges

Wilderness First Responder training was the experience of a lifetime. When I think back to that final simulation where people were struck by lightning, stung by bees, severed by fallen trees, and scared out of their minds, I can't help feeling incredibly lucky. It had been one of the most uncomfortable and terrifying situations of my entire life, because the instructors created the condition in our mind that all the rescues were real. I pushed myself in a way that I had never known. If I didn't make it through all of the discomfort, if I didn't push myself past my own boundaries, I'd still be the same scared communication nerd who lacked real confidence and the ability to tie knots.

For most of us, it's like we are looking at the world through a tiny, little keyhole. As much as we try to see what's out there, we can't do it from behind the massive, locked door of our comfort zone that is right in front of us. Instead, we need to venture on the other side of the unknown to explore the uncharted, to experiment with the unfamiliar, and to play with mystery. Exploring and playing with our comfort levels in this way can help us overcome the fear of public speaking, spark creativity, foster leadership, lessen unhealthy stress, boost productivity, improve memory, increase learning, multiply social circles, cultivate compassion, gain a sense of gratitude, and in some cases, may even encourage us to start our very own businesses.

Surprisingly, there's a great deal of research on the idea of taking risks and experiencing discomfort for positive growth. First up, we have *Optimal Anxiety*, which means that the brain requires a little bit of anxiety or stimulation in order to learn, grow, become more productive, and perform at a higher level[1]. The entire Wilderness First Responder training was built on this idea. The trainers threw us into all kinds of controlled, stressful situations in order for us to learn the material in an unforgettable way. This kind of healthy stress has been touted for over a hundred years and is found in classrooms, training sessions, and workplaces all across the world[2]. I like to think of it as the "Let's see what happens" approach to everyday living. I wonder what it would be like to try out a new recipe tonight? *Let's see what happens*. What if I just walked in and asked my boss for a raise? *Let's see what happens*. I'm curious to know what would happen if I quit my job and started my own business. Well, *let's see what happens*. At its very core, this approach is about exploration, experimentation, and ultimately having fun while maximizing life's potential.

Next up, we have *Cognitive Behavioral Therapy*, which means that we can use our brain and the way we think about things in order to change our behavior in the future[3]. This approach is all about the relationships between how we think, how we act, and how we feel. The underlying assumption of this technique is that "our *thoughts* cause our feelings and behaviors, not external things, like people, situations, and events"[3]. In other words, if we change how we think, then we can change how we behave and feel. This type of therapy is primarily done with a licensed professional, but it serves as a helpful framework to understand how we can pay more attention to the way we think, in order to change other parts of our lives in a positive way. When I was in my Wilderness First Responder training, I experienced thoughts of self-doubt and felt that I was not good enough to save people. Over the course of the week, I developed new patterns of mind that resulted in new, courageous behavior, ultimately making me feel more capable and confident.

Finally, we have the not-so-scientific foundation for challenging our comfort zone and trying new things, it's called *Curiosity*. As it turns out, curiosity is something that we share with several other animals. Monkeys, cats, dogs, foxes, rats, crabs, bees, ants, and even worms have been found to explore unknown objects and navigate new territory, not just for survival, but for information as well[4]. While it may not be surprising that monkeys, cats, and dogs utilize curiosity as an everyday tool, most people look shocked when I tell them about the curious worm, but it is true. When a roundworm is dropped on a petri dish, it will stay local for about 15 minutes, then it will head in a clear, new direction to gather more information about the environment[5]. Perhaps this might have something to do with all the positive benefits from the "Let's see what happens" approach.

At a neurological level, when we are curious, we activate the parts of our brain that are associated with learning, memory, and reward[6]. Not only does exploring help us understand new information, it also enhances the entire learning process, and, ultimately, helps us retain valuable knowledge down the road[7]. This is why the field of education has talked about the importance of curiosity for children, teens, and even adults for so many years[8]. Researchers believe there are gaps in every person's knowledge and information about the world, and curiosity is the tool that we use to fill them[9].

Above all else, curiosity has kept us alive for thousands of years. What happens if we chisel the end of this stick down with a rock? We get a spear. What happens when we poke a giant bear? They get angry and try to eat us (good to know). And how about if we put these little beans and seeds in the ground and see what happens? Well, look at that, an abundance of food grows right up from the dirt. When I was three years old, I wondered what would happen if I put my hands on the wood stove in the living room. Ouch! My first words became, "hot... hot, hot, hot!" I've gone the rest of my life with a keen eye toward hot things.

Thankfully, over one million years ago, some of our mildly brilliant ancestors had a similar inquisitiveness toward hot things. They played with flint and wood, which sparked the first documented fire in history[10]. Now, several centuries later, we are exploring Mars, engineering clean water, and even inventing stools to prop our feet up while we do our business in the bathroom. A delightful array of inventions have come as the result of accidental curiosity, including: pacemakers, microwaves, penicillin, inkjet printers, x-ray images, potato chips, and delicious chocolate chip cookies[11]. This is all because people have been, and always will be, curious.

Take it from NASA; after sifting through 9,000 student entries for what to name their newest rover, they chose "Curiosity" because it represents "the passion that drives us through our everyday lives"[12]. The student who submitted the name went on to say,

"Curiosity is an everlasting flame that burns in everyone's mind. It makes me get out of bed in the morning and wonder what surprises life will throw at me that day"[12].

Curiosity is such a pivotal part of our everyday life that scientists have used all kinds of words to describe it, including *information-seeking, learning, reinforcement, play, exploration, experimentation, neophilia* (someone who is interested in new things), *novelty, behavior flexing, flow,* and *a desire for new understanding*[6]. At a fundamental level, curiosity has been described as internally motivated information-seeking[6]. If we break this down, we find that *intrinsic motivation* really means doing something because it excites us or because it is enjoyable, and *information-seeking* means exploring[13]. For our purposes then, we can think of curiosity as *exciting exploration*. By challenging ourselves with the comfort challenges in this book, we have the opportunity to engage in this kind of exciting exploration, ultimately opening us up to learning new things, improving our brains, meeting new people, inventing revolutionary tools, and increasing our chances of survival.

It's important to note that growth happens when we step slightly out of our normal routines, but if we step out too far, too quickly, it is likely to cause a negative reaction like shock or panic. For example, if we're scared of heights and we decide that our first step is to jump out of a plane, we are likely to experience anxiety and fear, ultimately relapsing as an outcome[14]. A more strategic first move would be stepping up onto a curb or a small bench.

It's also important to note that everyone's comfort level is different. For me, public speaking was absolutely terrifying when I was younger. For some, it's not a big deal. For some people, smiling at strangers can be pretty tough. For others, leaping from the side of a mountain in a squirrel suit is nothing. The idea is that we all have a different baseline, and it's important to recognize where it is before we begin. The goal throughout this book is to excite and inspire you to try new things, to play with what life has to offer, and to experiment with the unfamiliar, all the while remembering to never tip the scales too far. As you navigate through this book and through the various missions and challenges, it is important to remember to take it slow, and move at a pace that doesn't strike up too much anxiety or fear. Again, if you are experiencing a real phobia, a debilitating fear, or overwhelming anxiety, then professional help is always the best option. If, instead, you are seeking personal growth in a fun, playful way, then this book is perfect for you.

Curiosity can lead to lasting change. For example, Einstein is famously quoted for talking about insanity, and how it is really just the idea of doing the same thing over and over, but expecting different results. When we think about the things we really want in life: a loving partner, a close family, everlasting happiness, a great job, a fancy car, a dream house, more time, more fun, or more excitement, how can we expect to achieve any of those things if we are doing the same things over and over, and aren't doing something right now that helps us head in that direction? Think about it, waking up at the same time, driving on the same roads to the same job, going to the same bar after work, drinking the same drinks, and hanging with the same friends creates a feedback loop. To imagine that anything might actually change would literally be *insanity*! Instead, if we apply the "Let's see what happens" approach, one might decide to skip the bars after work and instead go to a concert. At that concert, while having the time of their life, they might meet someone extraordinary. Years pass, they fall in love, get married, travel around the world… well, you get the idea.

There's an infinite amount of extraordinary possibilities when we unlock the keyhole and push past our giant door of discomfort. Consider this book your controlled setting. The world has become your research lab, a place where you can take small risks in order to stimulate your life toward infinite, unpredictable opportunities. The door is right in front of you. The key is now in your hand. It's time to unlock what life truly has to offer.

Comfort Challenge 1: Baby Steps

Now the time has come for you to pull off your very first comfort challenge. Think of something that will make you *slightly* uncomfortable for this first one, as it is a baby step. It doesn't really matter what it is, as long as during the process you feel some discomfort.

While you are going through the experience, it is important to remind yourself that it is natural and absolutely okay to want to stop early or give up. The goal is to simply try. No matter how far you get, recognize that if you take the first step, then you are on your way to unlocking that giant door of discomfort in front of you. So, start small, have fun, and enjoy the ride!

Can't think of what to do? Try one of these ideas out:

- Try a new food
- Smile at five strangers
- Lay down in public for 30 seconds
- Take a cold shower

2

Welcome to Iceland

With a huge smile on my face, I pushed a pair of glass doors open and stepped outside. Immediately, a freezing and pervasive wind wrapped around me and squeezed, like the coiling of an ice-cold, venomous snake. My beanie blew off the top of my head, and my skin felt like it was instantly blistering. I hurried to where my beanie had fallen, picked it up, and stuffed it back on top of my head as quickly as possible. It was hard to tell if I was cold, wet, or dying. My smile turned to panic, and I ran back inside. Immediately, I was blasted by the warmth of the building as I ran through the doors. Bending over and taking huge breaths, I wasn't sure what to do next. My friend was waiting for me in the parking lot a couple hundred feet away. The airport I was in was straight out of a history book. No automated doors, no security cameras, no free Wi-Fi, no cell phone reception, no public computers… It was like technology had been hibernating for a lifelong winter. I walked up to the doors again, held my hands up to the glass, and peered out. Everything was coated in white. The curb, the sidewalk, the street, the building, and the cars in the parking lot all had a layer of snow nestled on top. I squinted hard and could see a sign off in the distance. It was blurry from where I was standing, but I could just barely make out the words. In twisted, whimsical letters, it said, "Welcome to Iceland."

I decided to put my oversized backpack down and take out extra layers. I rummaged through the main compartment and pulled out a fur hat that had earmuffs hanging down from the sides, a flannel scarf that looked like it belonged to my grandfather, and a pair of snowboarding gloves to wear over my not-so-warm mittens. I wrapped the scarf around the bottom half of my face, pulled the fur hat down to my brows, and slid the bigger gloves over the smaller ones. I threw my pack over my shoulder, clapped my hands a couple times, jumped up and down, and shouldered my way through the doors again. This time, as the wind and shivery air tried to take me down, I was better prepared. It reminded me of a great lesson I learned once, "There's no such thing as bad weather. Only bad preparation." Although, if there was such a thing as bad weather, this was it.

I huffed and puffed all the way to the tiny, rusting Volkswagen Golf that waited for me in the parking lot. Reaching for the door, I grabbed the handle and pulled. It didn't budge. My hand shook back and forth as I pulled the lever. The cold snuck in through my pants and caused my legs to tremble. I pounded on the window with my oversized gloves and shouted, "Let me in!" Erika, my ex-boss and friend in the driver seat, laughed with a devilish grin. She was a strong, stout woman with thick, brown hair. The freckles sprinkled throughout her face complimented her bold personality and blunt sense of humor. She was several years older, but just as tall as me. If it came down to it, though, she would win in a fight between us. "Come on! I'm freezing!" I yelled again. It was so cold that the water streaming down my face from my eyes nearly froze. After a few seconds, Erika finally leaned over and popped the door open from the inside. Before I could yell at her, I stuffed myself inside the car as fast as I could, praying she had the heater on. She laughed and said, "That's what we call a warm welcome from the land of ice." She chuckled again, then we jetted off down the road.

We were driving for about 45 minutes when the car sputtered, jerked a few times, and came to a complete stop on the two-lane highway. For the next two hours, we were stuck. Unfortunately, we had rented our car from some random guy who ran a questionable rental company from his apartment, which meant help was not easy. Erika pulled out her satellite phone and dialed the number of the young man we rented the car from. It turned out that he was away visiting his girlfriend in Paris, so he had to call his best friend to come help us. Meanwhile, I was grumpily whispering to myself that we should have rented from a reputable company, instead of from some sketchy dude.

Finally, two cars pulled up to us. A young man with brown hair, a pair of overalls, and a wool sweater stepped out of an oceanic blue Subaru, while a young woman with blonde hair, a pair of snow-pants, and an overcoat exited a peppered gray Subaru. The young man hurried over to us, apologizing profusely in his Icelandic accent, "I'm so sorry about my friend Arnar, he can be such a blundering dolt sometimes. I'm his best friend, Johann." He reached his hand out to shake mine. Then, he continued, "He probably shouldn't be running a rental car business, he's always so busy, and he's so forgetful," Johann rolled his eyes as he spoke, "Anyway, he called me and told me you were stranded. I don't work for him or anything, but the thought of two non-natives stuck out here in the cold was enough for me to help. Sorry it took so long, we live a couple hours away." He pointed to the girl next to him, "This is Katrin, my fiancée. We brought both of our cars so you can take one and we'll take the other back home. We'll leave his crappy clunker here for him to deal with when he gets back." I couldn't believe what I was hearing. These two friends had offered to go completely out of their way to help us. Not only that, they were offering up their car to us, even though they officially had nothing to do with Arnar's supposed "rental company."

After thanking them for their help, we drove off in Johann's oceanic blue Subaru. Thankfully, the ride was much smoother and it was better insulated, so it was also much warmer. I joyfully cheered, "Thank God we have a Subaru now! These things are built like tanks. There's no way we'll break down again." Erika glared at me and quipped, "Don't jinx it."

After driving for a couple hours, we curved off the main road and down a dirt ravine to a geothermal hot tub. These naturally heated ponds of water were scattered throughout the entire country and were known as "hot pots." We parked a few feet from the edge of the water, and got out of the car. I wrapped a towel around myself and slipped into swim trunks, the same way I would change before heading out to surf. I untied my oversized boots, took off multiple layers of socks, and pressed my bare feet onto the frozen blades of grass below. It felt like a bed of icy glass, and my feet went numb in less than a few seconds. I hurried over to the spa and jumped in. Like the flip of a switch, my entire body seared with heat. All the cold parts burned. My toes tingled and pulsed. A couple minutes later, after adjusting and soaking in the cozy warmth, I was the happiest I had ever been.

Time became an illusion. I wasn't sure if it had been minutes, hours, or days that we sat there. The sky was dark now, and the temperature had dropped significantly. We finally decided that it was best if we kept making our way toward our first hostel. Erika lifted herself out of the spa, wrapped a towel around her waist, then headed toward the car. I stood up, shook off some of the cold, then sunk back down into the warmth, not ready to leave it behind. "Come on Kevin, let's go," she yelled. "Fine," I replied with disdain. I grabbed my towel, nuzzled my head inside it, and shook with all my might. Then, I ran to the car as fast as possible and lay down in the backseat to change. "Don't look, I'm changing," I said. With laughter, she replied, "Don't worry, it's so cold it's not like there's anything to see." "Ha, ha, ha, very funny."

Bundled in my warm clothes, I sat in the front seat and closed the door. "Alright," I said with excitement, "Let's do this thing." I reached over to the center console and turned all the dials so that the heat would blast on when the car started. She put the keys in the ignition, cranked them over, and fired up the engine. Except, nothing fired up. The engine whirred and struggled to turn over. She cranked the keys again.

Same thing, the motor whined and moaned. "Come on, you stupid thing, start!" Erika yelled. I closed my eyes and prayed that it would. My body shivered as the cold seeped in through the closed windows. I realized I hadn't eaten since my free meal on the flight, which was several hours ago. I looked around the backseat, pulled open the glove box, checked the side door, but there was no food anywhere. My stomach rumbled. The same stutter kept coming from beneath the hood. After what seemed like 400 attempts, she turned the keys and nothing happened. Not even the slightest sound. The car was completely dead.

Flashes of nightmares cycled through my mind. Will I have to stave off the cold by setting the car on fire? What if we starve? Would Erika resort to cannibalism if she was hungry enough? I assumed we would probably freeze to death inside that stupid rental car before we would starve. Then it hit me, we could actually die. This wasn't just a playful predicament, this was downright danger. There have been several stories of travelers who had an unfortunate situation that became an unfortunate tragedy. I hoped we wouldn't become one of them. We were miles from civilization, the temperature was below freezing, we didn't have any food, and our car was dead. The beautiful and somewhat haunting thing about Iceland was that travelers could drive for miles and miles without seeing any buildings or homes or people. Luckily, we had seen a tiny village on our way here. Unluckily, it was miles away.

Erika kept cranking the keys, trying to start the engine. Nothing happened. Which also meant there was no heat in the car. My teeth were chattering and I was losing my composure, "What are we going to do? We don't have any food and we can't sleep in here, we could freeze to death!" She punched the dashboard and angrily replied, "I guess we'll have to walk." I whined, "But the town must be at least three or four miles away!" She shot me a stare, "Do you have a better idea?" With no other options, it was our only chance to survive. I reached to my pack in the backseat and pulled out pretty much all of my clothes. I shoved three layers of shirts over my body, two extra pairs of pants over my legs, a second scarf over my neck, and a beanie underneath my fur hat. I don't think a person could be wearing more clothes than I was at that moment.

My eyes were the only parts of me that were visible, and I imagined they glowed in the dark light like mini moons. Erika also stuffed extra clothing on, and grabbed our only flashlight, which, thankfully, had working batteries. We stepped out of the car and immediately, I was brought back to my experience of leaving the airport just a few hours earlier. Chilling wind swept around my body while a light snowfall placed ice crumbs on my clothes. I put my hands up to my mouth and blew into them, trying to warm my face up. We walked up the dirt path and onto the main road. There was not a car in sight. Cold wind continued to sweep and freeze my bones. I cursed the fact that we came to Iceland during the least busy time of year. Sure, I saved money, but dying was not worth it.

After what felt like the endless trek to Mordor, we finally approached a tiny village. (And when I say, "tiny village," I mean there were literally only five houses.) By the time we arrived, it was the middle of the night, my face was numb, my hands were freezing, and my toes had lost feeling. Only one house had a porch light on. We approached the door and knocked hopefully. Nothing happened. We knocked again. Still nothing. This time, I pounded my cold fist as hard as I could. We waited. After a few seconds, the door creaked open, revealing a plump man with a draping, hoary beard. A waft of warm air swept out from his home, bringing the tantalizing scent of bacon along with it. My stomach grumbled. I was convinced that I had already died in the car and this was heaven. Then the man grunted, and I instantly realized this was as real as it gets.

"Excuse me, hello... we need your help. We are stranded way down the road, our car is broken down, and we are stuck. Can you help us?" The man stared back at us. Holding his crusting and mustard-colored door, he grunted and nodded. He twisted his head in confusion, scratched his beard, and answered with a deep, raspy voice, "Hallo... uhmm, I sorry... um... err... no English... sorry." He bowed his head as a sign of apology. I felt defeated. I looked at Erika and she, too, had a face of despair. Then, a light bulb went off in my head. I turned to the man and held my finger up as if to say, "Wait, one second." Then, like a game of charades, I began acting out what had happened to us. I pretended to grab hold of a steering wheel, and pushed my foot on an invisible gas pedal. He nodded along. A few minutes passed of this charade-based conversation.

Eventually, the grizzly man gave us a thumbs-up, waved us in, and we sat down on his ripped, antique couch. The entire home smelled like a Thanksgiving dinner, complete with a roasted turkey and sweet cinnamon stuffing. The big man grabbed his phone, dialed a number, then began speaking in Icelandic to someone on the other line. After a quick conversation, he came back over and gave us another thumbs-up. Then, he poked around his kitchen, fumbled with a couple mugs, poured us tea, and brought us plates with an array of home-cooked food. We gorged like vultures. I couldn't believe this man's generosity. We were complete strangers and he let us into his home, fed us, gave us tea, and even called for help. His kindness not only filled us with warmth (literally!), but it also saved our lives.

A couple hours passed, and a man knocked at the door. He was the polar opposite of our host: stick-thin, clean-shaven, and scraggly from top to bottom. But, with an unforgettable entrance, he held up jumper cables. We cheered and hugged the man. We thanked our host, shook his massive hand, and jumped into the new stranger's truck. He drove us to our car without talking, since he too did not speak English. We popped the hood of the Subaru and he clamped the jumper cables onto the battery. Then, he revved his engine. In the stillness of the night, it roared like a lion. He gave a thumbs-up. Erika shoved the keys in the ignition, closed her eyes, and cranked. Nothing happened. She turned them again, but still nothing. I looked toward the man and put up my hands as if to say, "What's going on? It's not working." He shook his head and signaled that he wasn't sure why. He floored his gas pedal and, again, his truck growled loudly in the blackness. Erika took the keys out, waited a moment, then shoved them back in. She cranked. Nothing happened again. She shouted in frustration, "Kevin, you try!" Not sure what that would change, I decided it would be best not to tempt a beast during a temper. I sat down in the driver's seat, put my foot on the gas pedal, pressed slightly, and cranked the keys. This time, the engine roared to life. The sound echoed through the vast emptiness of the land. I smiled ear-to-ear, looked over at Erika, and just before I could gloat, she grumbled, "Don't you dare say a word."

We thanked the man for his incredible act of kindness and slipped him some cash for the trouble. He gave a big thumbs-up, hopped in his truck, and drove away. We got back in our car and did the same. Pulling up the dirt road, shifting into second, we sped off down the narrow two-lane highway.

Several days passed as we toured the eastern and northern parts of the country. We stayed in rickety hostels, slept on couches, accidentally stumbled into a microbrewery, took ferries to strangers' homes, hiked to icy waterfalls, jousted with oversized icicles, and explored the insides of Earth.

About halfway through our trip, we were heading further north to the highlands. Travel magazines refer to this part of the country as an "untamed mingling of rocky deserts, jagged peaks, volcanoes, ice caps, valleys and hot springs, that should be explored at all times with respect, care and preparatory measures"[1]. Unfortunately, I didn't read those travel magazines until after our trip. We didn't have any of the necessary measures, nor did we understand what we were getting ourselves into. Without cell phones, all-terrain tires, or snow chains, we embarked on a journey that would have been dicey, even for Indiana Jones.

Driving along the highway, we passed a small sign on the side of the road that said, "Welcome to the Highlands. Proceed with Caution." I glanced at Erika, scrunched my face, and said, "Uhh, why does it say 'Proceed with Caution' on that permanent sign?" She responded with confidence, "Probably because people don't know how to drive. Good thing I've been driving stick since I was a little girl. We'll be fine."

As we drove, the conditions outside shifted drastically. What started as a slight snowfall was now a sheet of white. It was hard to tell where the sky ended and the land began. At one point, I looked out the passenger window and all I could see was white. Literally. I couldn't make out any objects. I looked out the front windshield and started to panic. I couldn't see the road. All white. Everywhere. I could barely even see the hood of the car. I spoke up, "Erika, what should we do?" She chuckled with arrogance, "It's fine, Kevin. It's just a white-out. I've been through a million of these." I stammered, "But you can't see anything! Let's pull over and wait until the snow passes." She laughed again. "The snow doesn't just pass here. This is the highlands. In fact, it pretty much always snows up in this part of Iceland." She spoke like a seasoned travel guide.

Then a pair of headlights headed straight for us.

It happened in an instant. It was impossible to see the dividing yellow line on the road, and we had drifted into oncoming traffic. As soon as we saw the car heading toward us, Erika spun the wheel. Horns blazed through the blurry white backdrop. I reached up and grabbed hold of the roof handle. We both screamed. Our car slid back toward the correct side of the road, narrowly missing a truck that was in front of us. I was breathing like a maniac. My chest was heaving, and my heart was sprinting. Erika veered off the road onto the shoulder and stopped the car. "I told you we should have pulled over!" I yelled. She was breathing heavily too. Between breaths, she said, "That was way too close. Let's wait for a little while and see if the weather gets better."

For the next couple hours, we sat on the side of the road trying to keep ourselves busy while we waited for any color other than white to appear outside. We played cards, showed each other classic favorites from our iPods, and snacked on Icelandic yogurt. Finally, as we were running out of things to keep us busy, the sleet slowed down and decent visibility returned. We got back on the road and pressed on.

Snow was still falling and we were surrounded by white landscape, but at least we could see a few cars in front of us. As a hill approached, we inched our way up trying to prevent the tires from slipping. It felt like the chain-link start to a rollercoaster. It dawned on me that I hadn't seen another car on the road for several miles. In fact, I don't think I had seen a car since the second road sign we passed that said, "Dangerous terrain ahead. Proceed with Caution." But I trusted Erika. She was older, and she had traveled all over the world before this.

The hill flattened and we were treated to one of the most spectacular views I had ever seen. Glorious white mountains cascaded in the distance. If I squinted, I could see the foam-tipped waves of the ocean far off in the background. To our left, there was a deep canyon of jagged, volcanic rock. To our right, there was a snowy trench. At this point, I understood the sign I had seen earlier. If anything were to happen with our car here, it would most likely mean death. We slowly moved across the peak of the hill. "Nice and easy," I suggested. I could feel a deep nervous sensation in the pit of my stomach. It felt like the breath-taking moment on a rollercoaster, just after the chain-link ascent, and just before the big drop. Time stopped. I could hear the wind dancing and swirling around our car. Then we dropped.

The hill descended and took our car with it. At first, it was a slow slide. Then, we picked up speed and started sliding faster. Erika tried to pump the brakes, but our car kept sliding. Erika mumbled to herself, "Oh shit, oh shit. Oh God. Come on, you stupid thing. Come on!" I yelled, "What's happening?" She kept slamming her foot down on the brake pedal. But we kept moving. I watched as she yanked the emergency brake, and for a split second, the car felt like it was slowing down. Then, the tires locked, and we kept sliding quickly down the slick, icy road. She shook her head, "No, no, no, this is black ice." Right then, I realized I was helpless as the passenger. There was nothing I could do. I was stranded and trapped in a metal death mobile. If we slid off the road to the left, we'd end up tumbling into sharp, lava rock, which nearly guaranteed dying. If we slid off to the right, we'd end up sideways in a snowy trench, which had a slight chance of survival. Recognizing this, Erika spun the steering wheel as our car continued to drift down the mountain. The car twisted and slid in all different directions. I was screaming the entire time. I tried to close my eyes and take whatever was coming, but curiosity kept forcing me to look. We were sliding toward the rocky cliff when one of our tires dropped off the edge. This was the end.

As the tire clipped off the side of the cliff, it spun our car the opposite direction. Narrowly avoiding a fatal fall to the rocky bottom, we careened across the road back toward the right side. Then, in an instant, we glided off the highway and flew into the snowy trench. Everything stopped, including my breath. My body was shaking but the world felt still. A beeping sound came from the dashboard. It was a warning indicator that we lost traction. "No shit," I thought to myself.

I peered over at Erika. She was staring with hollow eyes and a shocked look on her face at the steering wheel. As I looked past her and out the driver side window, all I could see was white sky. The car was nearly sideways, so I couldn't see the road through her window. I gazed out my own window and realized that I couldn't open my door because the ground was in the way. Trying to lift the mood, I jokingly said, "A warm welcome from the land of ice, right?"

*   *   *

A couple hours passed and a wish came true. A search and rescue vehicle arrived with two Icelandic angels on board. Their truck resembled a bullet-proof tank, and their orange jumpsuits could be mistaken for prisoner outfits. They hopped out of their vehicle and assessed the situation. Moments later, they hooked the back of our car up to a steel cable on the front of their truck. They moved quickly, without any regard for danger. Erika climbed out of our car and I followed her through the driver door, since I couldn't get out on my side. I bundled up in my snow jacket and sat on the side of the road as I watched these two men save us. One rescuer jumped into the driver seat of our car, while the other put the truck in reverse. The next thing I watched absolutely blew my mind.

The man in the truck backed up until he was starting to go backward off the cliff that had the jagged rocks below. I yelled, "Hey! Hey! Stop!" Then, his truck went vertical and dropped. Instantly, our car was yanked out of the trench and onto the road in an upright position. The rescuer in our car revved the engine and spun the tires. This gave him enough momentum to pull the other man's truck back up over the edge and onto the road. The man in the truck hopped out, unhooked the steel cable, and ushered us to get into his truck. The other rescuer in our car started to slide down the road. I watched in horror as the tires locked again, but the car kept moving. It drifted without control. I tried to speak but found myself short of breath and lacking words. Erika sounded panicked as she spoke up, "Um, hey, is he going to be okay? He's drifting. Do you see that?" She pointed for our rescuer to look. To our surprise, he giggled. In broken English, he said, "This is our job." With grace and skill, the man in our car was able to drift all the way down the road to the bottom, although there were a couple close calls with the cliff. We met him at the end of the hill and thanked both of them endlessly. This had been one of the single greatest acts of kindness I had ever witnessed. These two men put their lives at risk to save ours. To properly thank them, we tried to tip them with cash. They declined and told us they were not allowed. Instead, we handed over a six pack of beer and a box of cookies. They smiled and gladly accepted. Then, they both cracked open a beer, took a sip, hopped in their car, and drove off. I stood there, speechless, and laughed as I said to Erika, "Isn't it ironic?" She looked at me confused, "Isn't what ironic?" I smiled and replied, "That they saved our lives by killing us with kindness." She rolled her eyes, "You're an idiot. Let's go."

The Science Behind
Acts of Kindness

K indness is an amazing thing. It can bring complete strangers together, strengthen communities, bring smiles and laughter to the most miserable faces, serve as a platform for friendship or love, diffuse rage, save lives, improve health, and also save you from certain death in the highlands of Iceland. Not only that, it can cost little-to-nothing, take little-to-no time, and yet, positively change the world. To illustrate this, it's about time we met a little boy with a big heart, and an even bigger community.

Nicky was a fun-loving Boy Scout from a small town in the Midwest. He was the kind of boy who mentored younger kids, had a great outlook on life, and was always willing to lend a helping hand. Surely with time he would become the classic hometown hero with the key to the city, beloved by women, revered by men, cherished by friends, and idolized by younger children. Tragically, however, Nicky was diagnosed with a rare type of terminal bone cancer at the age of 14. Nicky's biggest wish in the world before passing was to earn the highest rank as an Eagle Scout. His troop did everything they could to accelerate the process. They expedited paperwork, tackled small achievements, and accelerated good deeds. By the time Nicky was in a wheelchair, he had one last project before he could achieve the Eagle rank. But, the project was a big one: to build a cabin in the forest for educational purposes. He simply couldn't do it alone.

In an extraordinary display of kindness, his entire troop came together to work on the cabin. Then, other troops started to join in from nearby towns. Word spread, and members of the community came to help in any way they could. Family members, friends, and even strangers provided wood, materials, time, effort, and resources to help Nicky earn his final achievement; his one last dream. Amazingly, the cabin was built in record time and Nicky had done it with the help of his community. He had finished all of the projects to earn his rank as an Eagle! His troop master came over to his house late in the evening to sign paperwork and make everything official. The next morning, Nicky passed away. But, thanks to the compassion and kindness of his friends, family, troop, and community, Nicky will live on forever in our hearts as an Eagle, as a legacy, and as an inspiration of genuine human kindness.

Nicky's story is not the only act of kindness that tugs at the heartstrings. For example, in an announcement that shocked the world, the founder of Facebook, Mark Zuckerberg, said that he and his wife would be giving away 99% of their company shares to charity, in order to make the world a better place[2]. Johnny Depp, a famous movie actor, visited sick children in hospitals while dressed up like Jack Sparrow from Pirates of the Caribbean, just to make their days a little better[3]. Jack Johnson, a popular singer-songwriter best known for his laid-back, good vibes music, decided to give 100% of his world-tour proceeds to charities, because he believed that other people needed the money more than he did[4]. Christian Bale took time out to call a young boy that was diagnosed with leukemia because all the boy wanted before time was up was to meet Batman[5]. In a smaller act of generosity, Keanu Reeves gave up his seat on a packed subway for a young woman[5]. Despite their wealth, fame, and elite status, these actors, musicians, and CEOs gave back to the community in a powerfully positive way.

Celebrities aren't the only ones offering up their seats and doing good deeds. In fact, one Google search of "acts of kindness" yields over 28 million results, including various articles, news stories, blogs, research papers, photos, and videos dedicated to sharing stories of compassion and altruism. Some of the stories are moving and inspirational. Others are downright humbling.

For instance, John and Linda were a happy couple until, tragically, Linda had a stroke and could no longer read. Every single day after the stroke, John took her to coffee shops and tried to help her re-learn how to read through memory games and quizzes[6].

Frank, a security guard at Disney World who previously spent 35 years in the German navy, approached children who were dressed as famous movie characters and asked for their autograph while complimenting them[7]. The children literally skip away with happiness and joy, thanks to the magic of one part-time employee.

Cesar, a part-time mover for a company in Florida, was riding in an elevator that stopped moving during one of his jobs. There was an elderly woman who was also on the elevator, and she had difficulty standing, even with her walker-device. After some time passed, she literally couldn't stand any longer, so Cesar got down on his hands and knees, and told her that she could rest on him. For the next 30 minutes, he provided a seat for this woman by using his own body as a bench[8].

In Russia, fans at a concert lifted a young man in a wheel chair up above the crowd so he could have a chance to crowd-surf and actually see the band on stage. In America, dry cleaners have posted signs in their windows letting unemployed people know they could get their clothes cleaned for free, for interview purposes. In the Middle East, an Afghan man approached American soldiers during combat with warm cups of tea as a sign of hospitality.

If you are anything like me, then the stories and examples above probably give you chills, goose-bumps, smiles, or at the very least, a warm heart. Even after writing this section, editing it, and re-reading it several times, I still get a cozy, comforting feeling that genuine human goodness exists. While one explanation for this powerful response could be mirror neurons, which cause us to feel the emotions of other people[9], I believe there is a deeper trigger for compassion and kindness in our bodies, in our brains, and in our hearts: Kindness keeps us alive.

Compassion, kindness, generosity, and cooperation are all traits that increase our odds of survival. Some writers and researchers refer to this as the survival of the kindest[10]. While you might be thinking, "Hey, wait a minute, what about survival of the fittest?" It turns out that Darwin was actually a big fan of sympathy and compassion, noting that these traits helped our species flourish[11]. In other words, kindness has kept us alive for thousands of years, and continues to keep us alive to this day. For example, during the devastating 2010 earthquake in Haiti, the tragic 2004 Tsunami in Thailand, the disastrous 2008 wildfires throughout California, the horrific 2005 Hurricane along the Gulf

Coast, as well as most major natural disasters around the world, people shared food, water, and valuable resources to help their tribes survive[12]. Amazingly, during overwhelming, chaotic, and massive tragedies like the ones above, trivial things that separate us such as class, location, age, gender, and other demographic qualities start to dissolve and leave us with greater human connection[13]. Not only does this type of connection happen during natural disasters, it is also at the very core of human nature.

The moment we pop out of the womb, we need to be taken care of, by mothers, fathers, doctors, and our community. If we were left to fend for ourselves as babies, to scratch and fight and claw our way through the thickness of urban jungles, we would surely die. In fact, without kindness at birth, we would never make it past the first day.

If this isn't enough to make you a believer, perhaps some of the research and science behind the benefits of kindness will. One study found that after just 10 days of engaging in acts of kindness, people reported higher levels of life satisfaction[14]. Research also suggests that by doing different kind acts for different people over time, we can feel happier, more appreciated, and can generate more friendships[15].

Researchers at Harvard University discovered that kindness is what keeps us connected to others, in terms of resources and social support[16]. Scientists at the University of Southern California discovered that gratitude, in response to generosity, is not only good for our social well-being, it's also good for our brain. They discovered that areas in the brain linked to reward, goodwill, empathy, moral behavior, fairness, and positivity all lit up in response to kindness[17]. In fact, after taking a closer look, scientists believe that a specific part of the brain that extends through the body, is activated whenever altruism or care-taking occurs[18]. It is called the *Vagus Nerve*, which unfortunately does not include a slot machine, poker table, or white tiger show. It is believed, however, to spark a feel-good chemical in our body called *Oxytocin*, which is the same feel-good chemical that is released when we experience love and connection with others[18]. Simply put, when we do kind things for other people, it can make us feel like we're falling in love.

As if it weren't good enough already, kindness can also create a ripple effect of more generous behaviors from other people. The classic example of this is shown in the movie, *Pay It Forward*, where the idea is to do good things for people, and they will continue to do good things for other people. In one wildly true example, a Starbucks Coffee shop in Florida reported a chain of 378 customers who paid for the next person in line, which went on for a staggering 11 hours[19]. This is not the only example of contagious kindness. At a pizza shop in Philly, one customer offered to pay for someone else's pizza, but no one was in line behind him. The clerk created a free pizza voucher out of a post-it note, and hung it on the wall for someone to take advantage of in the future. Over the next year, more and more people joined in and added post-it notes to the wall by paying for future customers. To date, there has been over 8,000 slices of pizza given to others in a pay-it-forward fashion[20]. Similarly, JetBlue, an inspirational airline company, has implemented a program called "Flying it Forward." They offer exclusive, free flights to people who plan to spread good and "make the world a little better"[21]. Some of their passengers have offered up shoes to people in need, some have volunteered their time at hospitals, and one passenger started a dream project: recycling donated pillowcases and turning them into clothing for

Haitian orphans. By offering a few free flights, JetBlue has created widespread inspiration through generous acts of kindness.

The good news for us is that research supports this ripple effect of generosity. In a study with over 1,000 receivers of kind acts, the majority of them said they would pay it forward soon, and almost 40% of them had already done so[22]. Behavioral scientists call it the *Social Contagion Effect*, which is the idea that one person behaving in a certain way can lead to others behaving in the same way[23]. Furthermore, once a person sees several other people doing something in common, they are more likely to do that same thing, which scientists call *Herd Mentality* or *Social Proof*[24]. In an article featured in the Public Library of Science, researchers discovered that receivers of kindness, specifically, are more willing to be generous toward others, which supports the social contagion notion[25]. Not only that, kindness and cooperation have also been found to spread as far as three degrees of separation[26]. To illustrate this, imagine you bring a warm cup of tea to a stranger named Bill, who is in the cold. Bill then offers his jacket to a stranger named Sally. Sally then buys a warm meal for a homeless man named George.

Without planning on it, your small gesture of warm tea has rippled out, and has not only brought goodness to Bill, but also to George and Sally. While research directly supports at least three degrees of separation, most people argue there is no end to the spreading of kindness. We may not know exactly how it serves other people down the road, but we can be fairly confident that it will.

For those of you traditional-minded business folks, I bet you're probably laughing to yourself right now, thinking about how this kind of gushy, feel-good, lovey-dovey stuff would never work in the cutthroat world of business. But you'd be wrong. It has been found that people are actually more attracted to positive relationships and kindness at work, than merely the size of a paycheck[27]. People would rather have a community of positive coworkers than make more money. Specifically, 80% of 2,000 polled employees agreed they would turn down a big salary increase if it meant "working with people or environments they didn't like"[28].

Compassion and kindness are becoming so valuable in business that over a dozen scientists, business professors, and corporate experts held a Compassion &

Business conference at Stanford University to share their powerful findings. One expert, later published in Harvard Business Review, said that compassion and kindness promote a culture of trust, collaboration, and creativity, as opposed to toughness, which promotes a culture of fear[27]. Another expert and lecturer from Stanford University discovered that companies like Chipotle, Airbnb, and Under Armour all participate in compassionate acts for their employees, as well as for other businesses they team up with. In fact, when 200 top entrepreneurs were interviewed, one of the main findings was the role and importance of generosity in the workplace[29]. Compassion has become such an asset in business that the Stanford University Graduate School of Business implemented a course on Mindful and Compassionate Leadership, where they explore and discuss the nature of kindness and empathy in the workplace[30].

It's important to note that it is not always grand acts of generosity that lead to these results, but it can also be subtle or small acts of kindness that generate compassion and loyalty at work. The co-founder of LinkedIn made the suggestion that it's not about throwing yourself on a set of railroad tracks for someone else, but simply thinking about how to be useful for the people around us[28]. Kindness and compassion are now incorporated in the trainings of medical doctors, teachers, executives, board members, prison guards, and juvenile detention workers[18].

Kindness is pretty amazing. It is scientifically proven to keep us alive, make us happier, help us enjoy more of life, encourage us to be more charitable, infinitely spread without an end in sight, and can even be good for business. The best part is that we get to decide how big or small, how free or costly, and how challenging or easy it is. Imagine, if everyone did an act of kindness each day, we could actually make the world a better place.

Comfort Challenge 2: Act of Kindness

For this comfort challenge, you are invited to do an *intentional* act of kindness. While *random* acts of kindness have been getting more popular, our goal is to focus on being a part of the process, instead of doing it secretly. Intentional acts of kindness require us to be front-and-center during the action. Some examples include delivering an unforgettable compliment to someone, offering to help a stranger carry their groceries, gathering friends to do a park cleanup, thanking an employee for their hard work, or even giving a bottle of water to someone who looks thirsty. Regardless of what you decide to do, the goal is to serve in a positive way for the greater good of the community. It's time to turn compassion into action!

3

Saved by the Sandwiches

Soaring through the air at 36,000 feet, I reclined my seat back and tried to get comfy. I pressed the little button on the side of the arm rest, pushed back with all my might, and the seat went back about two inches. Thinking there had to be a way for it to go back further, I held the button down and thrusted my body back and forth against the chair until I finally realized that it wasn't going any further. I couldn't believe this plane was advertised as having more leg room! I rolled over onto my side and rested my head against the head-rest. Moments later, I rolled over to my other side and tried resting my head on my shoulder. Still uncomfortable, I unlocked the tray table, let it drop, then leaned forward and rested my head down on it. This was the worst yet. I put the table back up and tried lifting my knees to scrunch into a little ball. I shook my head, this was no good either. No matter what I did, I couldn't get comfortable. Great, only 14 hours to go.

Since I wasn't going to be able to nap or get any rest along the way, I thought my next best move was to strike up a conversation with the person next to me. I was once told that strangers are just friends we haven't met yet and that each new person we meet in life brings with them a whole new world of opportunities.

I turned to my right and looked at the person sitting next to me. He had sharp, black hair that was delicately combed over the top, and stuck straight up in the back where he had a cowlick. His face was a bit round, and he looked of Asian descent. He happened to be sleeping, although I couldn't imagine he was getting any rest on these uncomfortable seats. I tried to wait for him to wake up. A few minutes passed and I started to get really bored, so I poked him on the shoulder. He blinked his eyes open and looked at me groggily, "Yeah?" I didn't think far enough in advance for what to say back, so I lied and said, "What do you want to drink? Just so I know when the flight attendant comes by, I can order for you." He looked at me confused, and said, "I don't know, a Ginger Ale I guess." He started to roll back over. Wanting to keep the conversation going, I quickly replied, "Oh really? That's what I always drink on airplanes. It helps settle my stomach if there's turbulence."

Many more minutes passed with awkward conversation, but eventually we started to connect. His name was Tang and as it turns out, he was an undergraduate student at the same university where I was studying for my graduate degree. We, along with about 28 other students, were on a plane crossing the Atlantic Ocean heading toward Europe for a summer study abroad trip. I had never met him before and didn't even know he was part of our crew. He started telling me about how he wanted to become more adventurous as a result of the trip, and I told him that I was the perfect sidekick for him. Little did I know at the time, he would become my best friend in Europe and would go on every single adventure with me. While others would be drinking and partying late into the hours of the night and early morning, we would be hiking, exploring, discovering, pioneering, and charting the unknown!

Tang not only came along for every adventure, but he also inspired me to talk to new people in every country. In Barcelona, we met some locals who convinced us to go mountain biking up a huge summit to an amusement park at the top. In Switzerland, we met some cabin owners who taught us how to eat a true Swiss breakfast with just meat and potatoes. In Germany, we met some folks at a Biergarten who introduced us to Steckerlfish, which translates to fish on a stick, and pretzels that were bigger than our faces. In Prague, we met some strangers who told us about a really cool restaurant that was on top of a docked boat in the river. And in France, we met a stranger who literally saved our lives.

*　　　*　　　*

While staying in Paris, I felt the need to leave the perfume and glamour that was all around me. I felt suffocated by the big city and yearned for some wilderness and some excitement. I walked down from my hotel room to the breakfast buffet, which served mostly soggy yogurt and do-it-yourself cereal, and met up with Tang. "Hey man, I'm feeling like we should do something outside of Paris today. What do you think?" Always up for it, he responded, "Of course. What should we do?" I sat for a moment and tried to think if I had heard of anything worth checking out nearby. As we sat at our table, just the two of us, other students walked by and I could overhear them talking about their plans for the day. Some of them talked about going to Versailles, others talked about going to the Louvre museum. I honestly had no interest in either of those places; I wanted to see what kind of nature this country had to offer.

Then another student walked by and sat at a table alone. I hadn't met him yet and he looked so lonely just sitting there all by himself. I imagined what it must feel like to be thousands of miles from home with a group of people that don't really acknowledge you.

So, I walked over to his table and introduced myself. "Hey man, mind if my friend and I join you?" He looked up, instantly smiled, and said with excitement, "Sure, yeah, hey guys, my name is Seth." We introduced ourselves and made the regular small talk. I asked him what his plan was for the day and he told me he wasn't really sure. He was just going to take a bus around and check stuff out in the city. I asked if he'd be interested in a bit of an adventure, and his eyes lit up. Then he said, "Wait, have you guys heard of Fontainebleau? It's the bouldering capital of the world. There's a forest with a ton of big rocks that you can climb. It's supposed to be really cool." I looked over at Tang excitedly, then back at Seth. "How far away is it?" I asked. "It's only a 45-minute train ride and the train is only a few bucks. Some random people told me about it last night, but I didn't have anyone to go with so I was just going to skip it." I looked at both Seth and Tang with a flicker in my eyes. "Well, what do you say? Let's catch the next train!"

As we planned out the trip, one of my other friends overheard us and asked if he could join. His nickname was Minks. He was pale and slender, but assured us that he was outdoorsy. Of course we agreed for him to join. We decided that we would rendezvous at the lobby in 30 minutes to give us each enough time to pack and get ready. We were only planning on being in the wilderness for a couple hours, so it was agreed that we would pack light.

A half hour later, I met up with the crew. We tallied up our provisions. For food, I had a single carrot and a granola bar. Between the three of them, they had trail mix, some dried fruit, and a bag of candy coated peanuts. As for hydration, I had two plastic water bottles in my backpack, Minks had a 16-oz. canteen, Seth had a single water bottle, and Tang had a can of Pepsi. Clearly, we weren't all that prepared. Thinking on my feet, I said to the others, "Hey, what if we run back up to the breakfast buffet and take some food to go?" "That's a great idea, except it's probably not allowed," Seth replied. Minks stammered, "What if we get caught? Won't we get in trouble?" After a few moments of deliberation, we ran up to the buffet, discreetly shoved deli meats and pastries into our pockets, then ran back downstairs.

We looked like a team of adventurous misfits heading into the first chapter of a children's book. I was wearing an old brown shirt and a pair of grey shorts that no longer had the button to hold them together. Instead, I looped my belt extra tight, then just untucked my shirt and hung it over so that no one could tell. As for accessories, I had a ripped, floppy backpack that had no support, and a pair of shoes that I referred to as my 'ninja shoes,' which were really just black tennis shoes.

Minks had black gym shorts on that barely made it to his knees, a blue tank-top that was a bit snug, and white fleshy skin that stuck out from each arm and leg hole. His signature accessory was a brown, leather bracelet that looked as if a watch-face should be stitched in, but instead it just had a buckle and some holes. His backpack was dark forest green, which was perfect for blending in with the surroundings. He had glasses that hung a little low on his nose, so he always looked like he was going to point his finger at you and teach you a lesson.

Seth had a typical grey shirt that had the school logo on it, a pair of loose-fitting blue jeans, and a pair of black running shoes. Instead of a backpack, he had a cinch sack, which is one of those terribly uncomfortable bags that everyone at the gym seems to have. And of course, his sack also had the logo of the university on it. He was 'one of those guys,' - alumni for life.

Tang was the only one smart enough to bring a watch. Other than that, he also had a standard grey shirt on with a small pocket that had blue Hawaiian flowers, and blue shorts that were made out of the same material as big, comfy sweat pants. I couldn't help imagining how hot and sweaty it must have been up in there. Yuck. He had skate shoes and a messenger backpack that could also be altered to become a side bag. All-in-all, he looked more prepared for a short bike ride to the video game store, not for getting lost in the wilderness.

We left the hotel, made it to the train station, and hopped on the next train. For 45 minutes, I watched as the beautiful French countryside cascaded by out my window. Although everything was blurred from the motion, it was some of the most beautiful, vibrant greenery I had ever seen.

Once we arrived at the train stop, we realized we had to get to the forest. We made our way from the station, across cobblestone sidewalks and alongside stone houses, to the edge of town. The concrete faded into dirt and trees. We walked until we were deep enough in the woods that the brink of civilization could no longer be seen. I looked around at the gorgeous trees that soared up from the ground like pillars. I took a big breath and was treated to the delightful smell of wet soil and fresh air. The backdrop was like a luxurious terrarium for humans, covered with plants and trees of all sizes. I imagined my hazel eyes glowing green to match all of the scenery around me. I called out to the others, "Welcome home." I pointed to an empty space in the dirt, "This here is my den." Then, I pointed to another empty space nearby, "This area here is my living room, and over here behind this rock is the master bedroom, and if you follow me to this little hole I'm about to dig behind this tree, well, this is where we do our dirty business." The guys laughed, but to be honest, I was only slightly kidding. I really could have seen myself living in this place forever.

As we kept walking, Minks spotted a boulder that would be perfect for climbing. We scurried over to it and noticed there was a ledge that would require overhanging, which is when you go upside down while climbing. We all decided to give it a shot, even though we were pretty much out of our element. Minks went first, made it to the point where he hooked his heel over the rock, hung upside-down, panicked, and immediately came back down. Seth got pretty close, he climbed up, hooked his heel over, heaved and heaved, but couldn't get from upside-down to right-side up. Then Tang gave it a try. He made it about three feet up and came back down complaining that his hands were tired.

Then it was my turn. I dug my sweaty fingers into the rock, climbed up, hooked my heel over, swung back and forth to try to gain momentum, and just as I was ready to swing around and make it over the top, my grip slipped, my foot unhooked, and I came flying down. It felt like hundreds of feet as I fell, until I finally back-flopped onto the dirt. I immediately gasped as the wind got knocked out of me and rolled around in agony, until Seth pointed out that the overhang was only about five or six feet high. Embarrassed, I lied and told them I was choking on the carrot I had eaten earlier, that it had got shaken up during the fall. All three of them looked at me and laughed. In that moment, it struck me how three people who I didn't know just a week ago, and who I barely met within the past few days, had become some of my new favorite friends. I guess it's true that strangers are just friends you haven't met yet.

We realized the daylight was starting to give way as the sun was setting behind the clouds. We needed to find our way back to town and hop on the next train back to Paris. Thankfully, Minks was the only one smart enough to grab a map from the train station before we left. He pulled it out of his backpack and started unfolding it. A few moments later, his arms were stretched wide and the map overtook his whole body. No joke, from where I was standing, all you could see behind the map was his small hands, his two little feet, and the top of his glasses. This had to be the biggest map I'd ever seen. Minks asked if anyone had their phone with them and I raised my hand. "We can use the compass on it so we can use the map." Turns out, Minks was a great friend to have along as he was a previous Boy Scout.

I pulled out my phone, opened the compass app, and as luck would have it, it didn't work at all. The compass just kept spinning in circles. North, east, south, west, then back around, over and over. I tried everything I could, I swung the phone around in a figure-eight trying to recalibrate it, I lifted it up and down in a fanning motion, but nothing helped. We were out in the middle of a forest, in the middle of the countryside, in the middle of France, and we were lost.

We decided to follow a trail that looked like it was the most heavily used in the past. There were foot prints all over it, so we figured it must lead somewhere. Tang spoke up, "You guys, I'm getting pretty hungry." Seth agreed, "Yeah me too, I guess we should have brought more food, huh?" I tried to console everyone, "You guys, it has only been a couple of hours. We'll be fine. We can last days without food if we really need to." Minks shouted, "I don't know about you, but I'm really thirsty. And I'm not staying out here for days." Tang yelled back, "You're thirsty? All I had was a can of Pepsi today!" Minks shrugged, "Well, whose fault is that?" Just in time, Seth chimed in, "Guys, we're all pretty hungry and we need to find some water or a way out soon. Let's just keep walking."

So, we walked. For hours. We were thirsty, starving, cold, and lost. My feet felt heavy as I trudged along. I could feel the sweat from earlier hardening and drying out on my skin, making me colder and more uncomfortable. It had been several hours since any of us had anything substantial to eat or drink. I looked at the others and they looked hopeless. Seth was continuously rolling his eyes because he believed we should have went a different direction. Tang was rubbing his belly and licking his lips. Minks kept looking at his watch, then side-to-side, then back down at his watch. He looked back at me, then said, "You guys, I have some bad news." His head shook with worry, "If we don't make it back to the train station within the next hour, we won't be able to make it back to Paris tonight. And if that happens, we'll miss our bus to Germany tomorrow morning." Tang threw his arms up in defeat, "We're going to die!" I chimed in, "Hey, we're going to be fine. I'm pretty sure the train station is just a few more steps ahead."

Then, as we came around a corner of trees, we saw some lights in the distance. Minks shouted, "You guys, look over there! Kevin was right, we made it!" Except, I wasn't right at all. As we ran toward the lights, there was no train station. Instead, we found a medium-sized cabin nestled in the middle of the forest. Without a better plan, we approached and knocked on the door. No one answered, so I decided to see if it was locked. I grabbed the door handle, twisted, and pushed. Thankfully, the door opened. We crept inside, and to our surprise, it was some kind of restaurant!

Inside, the walls were lined with wooden slats, and farming tools were nailed up as decorations. The tables all had red and white tablecloths that made it look like a picnic hideout. A fireplace was lit and burning at the side of the room. The smell was warming and reminded me of my parent's wood stove back home. Suddenly, someone came out from the back-kitchen area and started speaking to us in French.

Considering my recent stroke of luck with meeting new people, I was excited to meet this new stranger. I said, "Hello sir, we're hungry and need food. We'd like to order something off the menu." He looked at me with a puzzled face, and continued to talk in French. Then he walked away back toward the kitchen. All four of us looked at each other. "So… should we leave?" I asked my friends. Seth said, "I'm not sure, I couldn't tell if he was upset or happy that we were here." Tang spoke up, "We should probably get out of here guys. It's no good if we can't speak their language." Moments later, the French man reappeared this time with another shorter man. The shorter man said, "Bon jour, err, hello, you speak English, yes?" I cheered, "Yes! Yes, yes, do you speak it too?" He replied, "A little. I'm sorry, we're closed. Come back tomorrow, yes?" I replied immediately, "No, no, you can't be closed. We haven't eaten a full meal all day, we're out of water, and we're a little lost. We have money, we would just like to buy some food."

Over the next few minutes, we chatted about how we came to go bouldering in the forest and how we got lost and didn't bring enough food or water. The man put his finger up, said "A-ha," then went back to the kitchen. He returned with four huge baguette sandwiches, complete with salami, pickles, and French cheese, and four tall water bottles. He put one sandwich and one bottle of water in each of our hands and said, "For you my friends. These are leftovers from the day. And to get to the train station, just walk out these doors, follow the trail to the left, and it will take you right to the town center. It's only a couple minutes or so from here." Seth yelled in the background, "I told you guys it was that way! We would have been home already!" I ignored him and reflected on this incredible act of generosity. A couple minutes ago, we barely spoke the same language. And now, this man, a stranger, was handing over survival nourishment and directions home. This man was no stranger, he was an angel!

We left the café in the woods and followed the trail that he suggested. Just a couple minutes down the road, we paused at a circle of rocks that made for a perfect pop-up dinner. We sat down, opened the wrappers to our food, and began to demolish the delicious sandwiches. Nothing had ever tasted so good in all my life. I spun the cap off the water bottle and chugged as fast as I could. It felt like liquid magic. Tang looked around and said, "You know, everyone else that's with us on this trip is over in Versailles, or at the Louvre museum, or whatever, but for us... this is all the art that we need." Jokingly, I agreed, "Yeah this is like real-life nature-Monet right here." Seth spoke up, "I triple that." Minks raised his hand, "I'll cheers to that." I looked at the wilderness misfits around me, smiled with absolute joy, and realized that strangers are literally just one adventure away from becoming true friends.

The Science Behind
Meeting New People

I t's amazing what a simple 'Hello' can do. In my own life, it has taken me around the world, saved my life on several occasions, helped me gain jobs with top-ranked companies, sparked the loving relationship with my girlfriend (soon-to-be fiancée), and even brought me the opportunity to publish this very book you are reading right now. Meeting new people can open infinite doors (and even windows), help you better understand yourself, help you better understand others, give you new ideas, and can even serve physical, practical, social, and identity-based needs[1]. In fact, the longest study that has ever been conducted on humans, which occurred for over 75 years at Harvard, had one major finding: Great relationships make us happier and healthier[2]. Above all else, when the participants were asked what mattered most after nearly a century, the majority mentioned something about their close relationships with other people being the single best thing life had to offer. In the beautiful words of a TED talk I recently watched, "When you talk to strangers, you're making beautiful interruptions into the expected narrative of your daily life and theirs"[3]. There are so many benefits it is hard to limit this section, but for the purpose of time and simplicity, let's just focus on three favorites: survival, opportunity, and confidence.

From a survival standpoint, our existence as a species has depended on our ability to work together with others. For example, the very notion of "hunters and gatherers" is fundamentally built on the premise that we need other people to stay alive. Imagine trying to live in isolation during a time with no advanced tools, no electricity, no technology, and nothing to help you except your own brain and body. Most of us probably wouldn't last a week, let alone a lifetime.

Popular media has toyed with this idea for years with stories like *Robinson Crusoe, Cast Away, I am Legend, Catch Me if you Can, Life of Pi, Interstellar, 127 Hours,* and *The Martian.* In all of these stories, the main character spends too much time alone and, as a result, becomes delusional. When people spend prolonged periods of time in isolation, they typically experience extreme emotions including rage, depression, angst, frustration, and ultimately, madness[4]. One case study involved a woman named Sarah Shourd who was put into an isolation prison for over 10,000 hours: "At one point, I heard someone screaming, and it wasn't until I felt the hands of one of the friendlier guards on my face, trying to revive me, that I realized the screams were my own"[5]. Without human contact, Sarah became mentally unstable, which is a common result of solitary confinement or isolation. This may be why one of the main models of human-needs says that just after food, water, and shelter, we need other humans to survive[6]. Don't just take it from me, take it from a neuroscientist who wrote an entire book about social connections: "Our need to connect is as fundamental as our need for food and water"[7]. In other words, our families, partners, and friendships are equally important as eating and drinking[8].

While my friends and I managed to stumble into some free sandwiches in the previous story, we very well could have become stranded and starving had we not met those French men in the woods. They played a vital role in helping us survive. There is no doubt about it. I would not be writing this right now if I hadn't had the help from a number of strangers all across the world. I've been rescued in Iceland, Mexico, France, and Spain, thanks to the kindness and support of other people. All of this is to say that the more people we meet, the more connections we make, and ultimately, the greater chance we have of getting help when we need it most.

From an opportunity perspective, relationships not only help keep us alive, they also help us grow. With each new person that we meet, there is a new skillset, new knowledge base, and new world of opportunity that becomes available. Our ability to secure jobs, achieve promotions, and experience joy is greatly increased when we build relationships with more people. For example, Forbes posted in a brief online article that 41% of jobs in 2010 were obtained by networking, which is a huge majority over the embarrassingly small 2% of jobs that were obtained via advertisement, or 8% from directly approaching companies[9]. We can be more strategic when looking for workplace opportunities by engaging with more people each day. In fact, one successful business book suggests that only 20% of our time should be spent on job boards, another 20% on building our resume and social media, and a whopping 60% on networking[10]. The days of cold-calls and walking into a business's main office with a resume in-hand are pretty much gone. That's not to say that we can't try, but current research suggests that our best bet is to build more relationships.

In my own life, almost all of the jobs and promotions I have achieved have come from talking with other people. Not only was I able to mow my neighbor's lawn when I was fifteen, I also scored positions with big companies like Apple, Sony Music Entertainment, Red Bull, Linux Foundation, and big universities like San Diego State University and National University, all from meeting strangers that eventually became friends. Perhaps it is best said by the co-founder of LinkedIn and his writing partner,

"Opportunities do not float like clouds in the sky. They're attached to people. If you're looking for an opportunity — including one that has a financial payoff — you're really looking for a person"[11]. Success is much more than just passion, luck, and hard-work, it is about our relationships and how we interact with others[12].

Fun fact: Facebook has a research team continuously crunching the data of their massive user-base to find interesting trends. As it turns out, based on 1.59 billion active users on the site, the average distance between any two people is about three and half degrees of separation[13]. What does that mean? We are connected to everyone in the world through only three or four other people. As you are reading this, there is a good chance that you know someone, who knows someone, who knows someone, who knows me. Which means, we might meet each other in the future! Inevitably, the more people we meet as we navigate through our lives, the more opportunities that will present themselves along the way.

Let's do some math for fun (I'm aware that math and fun are typically not used in the same sentence). Say you have 100 friends on Facebook. If each one of your friends has 100 friends, then your network is technically 10,000 people strong already (assuming your friends would introduce you to their friends if needed). Now, let's imagine you introduce yourself to one new person each day. Assuming you take a couple days off during holidays and stressful times, you'd meet about 300 new people in a year. If each one of those persons also has a network of 10,000 people, then you could potentially grow your circle of contacts to three million. After five years, that number would grow to 15 million. After 10 years? A staggering 30 million people. Now that's a lot of opportunity!

Talking to strangers can lead to all kinds of new opportunities and help keep us alive. But if you are anything like most people, including me, then introducing yourself to new people can be a pretty uncomfortable experience (which is why it belongs in this book!). All kinds of doubts and fears can run through the mind. What if we say the wrong thing? What if the person we meet thinks we're stupid? How could we possibly think of the right thing to say? Well, I have good news for us. The act of introducing ourselves to more people more often can help boost our confidence in socially anxious situations, which results in boosted confidence in other areas of our life as well[14]. While this is something that takes time, there's more great news. There is actually a pretty simple way to feel more confident with introductions.

One of the best ways to open a conversation is to talk about your shared situation[15]. When I went on my summer study abroad trip, I was nervous to talk to the person sitting next to me on the plane, so I just talked about the flight attendant and the free drinks that would inevitably take place. Other examples might be asking someone for a recipe at a grocery store, talking about how big a building is while you are in an elevator, requesting movie recommendations at a theater, or pointing at something that stands out in your environment. It's more important to actually start a conversation than it is to worry about the right thing to say. In fact, a nationally-known communication expert suggests, "Although many people sit around groping for the 'perfect' opener, research has shown that what you say is relatively insignificant"[15]. In other words, there's no such thing as a perfect opening. Just go for it and see what happens.

After the ice is broken, there are three simple ways to stir up great conversation and avoid the small-talk snooze.

One, make an attempt to find *surprising* things you have in common. In the last story, I found out the person sitting next to me went to the same school and was part of the same study abroad trip! Similarly, during a team-building training that I led, I found out one of the employees was best friends with the drummer of my band. I often have my students engage in this exercise and one semester, two of my students found out they were actually related! The moment a similarity is found between two people, a unique bond is created that makes talking to each other much easier.

The second way to stimulate great conversation is to try to find out *amazing* things about the other person. It is my belief that every single person on this planet has something extraordinary waiting to be uncovered. By asking the right kinds of questions, we can start to turn small talk into great conversation. These types of questions empower the other person to be as free as they wish with their response.

Here are some examples of engaging open-ended questions:

- How do you like to spend your time?
- What was a highlight from last weekend?
- What are you looking forward to most right now?

These types of questions are much better approaches to great conversation than dreadfully boring clichés like:

- What do you do?
- What city are you from?
- Do you like to sleep?

By asking more interesting, open-ended questions, it puts the spotlight on the other person and allows them to shine. One way to take this a step further is called a *conversation sparker*, which is a thought-provoking question that requires the responder to be creative and imaginative. Here are some examples of conversation sparkers:

- If you had tomorrow off, what would you do?
- Which 30 seconds of your life would you relive?
- Where would you go if you could go anywhere?
- What would you buy if you won the lottery?
- Which superpower would you choose and why?

These types of questions allow the responder to dream and desire, which puts them in a playful and enjoyable mood. No matter where I go, whether a professional mixer or a beachy gathering, I often use conversation sparkers as a way to stimulate unforgettable conversations with new people.

The third way to generate great interactions is to talk about things that *stand-out* around you. Maybe a tree has beautifully colored flowers or someone is walking by with a pizza box balanced on their head (this actually happened). This method takes the focus off you and the other person, which helps relieve any awkwardness that might be expected. Also, by experiencing something in common together, it creates a *confluence*, or a merging flow between you and the other person. Naturally, this makes conversation easier and more enjoyable.

To recap, the next time a conversation starts to fizzle, spark it back up by trying to find a *surprising similarity*, something *amazing* about the other person (open-ended questions & conversation sparkers), or something that *stands-out* in the environment.

Considering that our world is becoming more connected and easier to meet new people, you now have the tools to take advantage of the endless opportunities in front of you and feel more confident meeting more people. In fact, if you do the math, over a lifetime it can lead to more than 200 million opportunities. So, what are you waiting for? It's time to see what a simple "Hello," can do you for you.

Comfort Challenge 3: Meet New People

For this comfort challenge, you are invited to strike up a conversation with someone new. The goal is to talk for a minimum of three minutes, but if that is easy for you, then push to five, ten, or even fifteen minutes. Try to move past small talk and actually feel a connection. Notice things like eye color, hair color, clothing, voice tone, and other personality traits. Try to get their name if you can. The great thing about this exercise is that you can do it every single day with different results. Great places to tackle this challenge include grocery stores, lines for popular eateries, record shops, clothing stores, the mall, airplanes, buses, trains, etc. When you are seeking out a new person to talk with, be mindful of your safety. If they look sketchy and give you a bad vibe, then I'd recommend staying away. Otherwise, spark up a conversation and see what happens!

4

Downward Doggy Style

There were bodies everywhere. They lined the floor like the aftermath of a massacre, which made the hardwood beneath barely visible. Scents of body odor and lavender swirled in the air and created a unique mixture of serenity and sacrifice. The lights in the room were all off. Only the flicker of candles could be seen, which were magnified and multiplied by the mirrored walls. I was on the floor, nearly passed out, with sweat pouring down my face and body. The bodies next to me were breathing like they were held underwater for too long. It sounded like they were near death. Suddenly, a booming voice echoed throughout the entire room, "And now... corpse pose."

*   *   *

It was a day just like any other. My best friend, Torrin, and I were in our teens, having some fun, and getting into trouble. We were at a grocery store, rearranging items to mess with all the shoppers, when my pocket started to buzz. I pulled out my phone and saw that I had a text from Nate, another friend of mine. He was the kind of guy who loved to drive out to the desert to shoot paintball guns at lizards, considered himself an aviation specialist, drove a lifted off-road capable truck, smoked weed by the grams, drank beer by the dozens, and loved to go from one woman to the next. All in all, he considered himself a "manly man." Which is why his text shocked the hell out of me, "Hey man. Wanna try out some yoga later?"

I read the words and literally couldn't hold back laughing right then and there. I showed the screen to Torrin, and he reacted the same way, with a great big laugh. Just to mess with Nate, I wrote back sarcastically, "Heck yeah man. Right after we get a pedicure and swing by the salon." Only a few seconds passed and he responded, "No, I'm serious. Have you ever tried it? It'll change your life." Thinking this was just a big joke, I continued to respond comically, "Yeah, but my life's pretty great right now. I don't know if it needs to change." He persisted, "I said the same thing until I tried it the other day. It'll be free cause they have a week unlimited trial for new students." So, I coyly texted, "If it's so great for you, why do you want me to go so badly? Why not just go yourself?" Torrin nodded in agreement, letting me know that it was a good response.

Moments later, another buzz, and the text read, "Because I'm your friend. And friends help friends get better at life. That's what we're here for. So, if you were my friend, you'd come tonight." Everything in me wanted to say, "No," but damn, he had a good point. I looked to Torrin for help with what to do. Then I had a great idea. I'd get him to come with me, and we could make a big game out of it and get a huge laugh. As the next words came out of my mouth, Torrin immediately started shaking his head as if to say, "No… No, no, no. No way in hell. I'm not going with you." "C'mon man, it'll be super funny. Think about it, everyone's gonna be doing hilarious poses. It's like free entertainment!" So, despite both of us not wanting to go, and wanting so badly to say, "No," to Nate, we agreed that it'd be worth challenging ourselves. So, we went.

As we pulled into the parking lot of the studio, I got another text from Nate. "Hey dude, not going to make it tonight. See you next time!" A range of emotions fired through me. I blasted off a text right away, "What the hell?! What about all that stuff about being a good friend and being there for each other? We just drove 20 minutes to get here!" Rather dully, he replied, "Yeah, sorry, I just got some stuff I gotta do." I looked to Torrin for consolation. "What should we do?" He studied the situation. "Hmm, well… we're already here. And we drove pretty far to get here. I don't know, I guess I'm in if you're in." Again, the immediate response in my head was a huge "NO," but I figured it was worth a shot since we had come all this way and didn't really have anything else to do. "Alright, let's just go check it out. If it's that bad we can leave. And if it's really, really bad, then we can just make a bet to see who can make the funniest sounds when we do the weirdest poses." Just like kids, we high-fived and agreed.

As we walked into the studio lobby, it was immediately apparent there was nothing funny going on inside. The intoxicating smell of lavender essential oils fluttered throughout the lobby, and the lighting was tranquilly dim. If I could have chosen anywhere in the world to take a nap, it would have been right there. The petite girl behind the front desk said, in the most peaceful and spiritually warming voice I had ever heard, "Hi. Welcome to our beautiful studio, gentlemen. Have you two been here before?" Shrugging and chuckling as if to deny that we even stepped foot inside a yoga studio in the first place, "Us? No, no, this is all new to us. Are men allowed in the upcoming class? I don't really know anything about yoga, you know?" She smiled and said, "Of course. All are welcome here. Yoga is for everyone, short, tall, man, woman, and everything in-between. Let's go ahead and get you signed in."

She continued to walk us through the waivers and registration info to get us signed up for the class. Then she asked, "Do you have your own mat or will you need to borrow one?" I looked at her quizzically, "A mat? For what?" Chuckling, she responded, "In yoga, we use a mat for nearly all of the postures in order to give you support through the bodily progressions."

Confused, I responded, "Oh, okay, well yeah, I guess we'll need to borrow mats then."

Once all the registration was done and the mats were handed over, she informed us that our class would be held in the big room to the left, the Serenity Room, as she called it. I stopped at the men's locker room, which looked more like a Zen garden with a couple sinks and bamboo cupboards. I changed my pants into a pair of swim trunks and took my shoes off. I wondered, "Do I wear socks or go barefoot?" Hmm. I stood for a while as I deliberated. I decided the safest bet was to wear socks. If I wasn't supposed to, then someone would say something and I could just take them off if needed. As I was putting my stuff away and closed the cabinet door, I noticed a flyer on the wall that read, "Like Doggy Style? Then you'll love our upcoming workshop on Downward Dog! Come learn the ins and outs of one of the most popular poses in yoga." I scratched my head. "Well," I thought to myself, "Tonight ought to be interesting." I headed out of the Zen garden locker-room and toward the studio doors.

As I slowly opened the door, I felt as if I was stumbling into a portal to a new world. Inside the studio, there were hardwood floors, flickering candles spread all across the room, a massive mirror that lined the back wall, a live musician with a keyboard toward the back corner, and a shrine at the center that had an array of rocks, more candles, an elephant sculpture, and a big statue of the big-bellied Buddha. Huge blasts of heat were coming through the air vents and engulfing the room in a sauna-like hotness. The scent was calming, a mixture of minty oils and bodily warmth. I immediately noticed that everyone was barefoot, so I quickly moved out of the way of the door and yanked off my socks. Turning around, I saw Torrin doing the same thing. He looked at me and started laughing. "Shhh," I put my finger up to my lips trying to contain my own laughter. "Okay, okay," he nodded. I scanned the room and tried to figure out where to place my mat, not sure if there was a rule about the spacing between each person. I spotted what looked like just enough space for both of us, and I pointed for Torrin to follow.

I rolled my mat out next to a massive man that probably weighed over 350 pounds. I figured there's no way he could judge me, so it'd be a great spot. Torrin rolled his mat out next to mine and we sat in silence as we looked around. I noticed that everyone seemed to already be doing yoga poses, even though the instructor hadn't entered yet and the class hadn't begun. One thin, bendy girl was putting her legs up over her head in what I imagine would be named the Pretzel Pose. Another lengthy woman was putting her leg up in the air as her body twisted in half and her other leg somehow found its way up in the air as well. A gentleman across the room was huddled up in a ball with his forehead digging into the mat. The bloated man next to me was laying on his back with his eyes closed as he was letting out a soft but distinctive, "Ommmmm" sound. I immediately felt like I was in a circus tent with all of the performers preparing for the big show. I looked over at Torrin as he rolled onto his belly and tried to bend his legs backward to touch the top of his head. He looked at me and whispered, "Pshh, yoga's not that hard."

That is, until the instructor entered. "Hi everyone. Welcome to our Vinyasa Flow style class. This is one of our faster paced classes that is designed to generate a lot of heat and a lot of strength. I hope you brought towels, cause we're not leaving until you've flushed out all the toxins from the past week. I'd like you all to begin in Child's Pose." Having no idea what a Child's Pose was, I looked around and saw everyone huddling up in a ball and pushing their foreheads into the mat, just like the man was doing earlier. So, I followed suit. "Great," the instructor called out, "Now we want to really get the fire flowing through our bodies. We call this Pranayama, or the breath of fire and life. We achieve this through Ujjayi breathing, which you can do by hugging your tongue to the back of your throat and breathing audibly." I didn't understand a word she said, so I just kept breathing regularly.

All of a sudden, everyone around me started breathing in a way that sounded like they were held underwater for too long. I knew I was supposed to be paying attention, and I tried to be more mindful, but I couldn't help imagining Darth Vader walking into the yoga studio and seeing everyone mimicking him with their deep breaths. I imagined he would be very upset, and he'd probably start light sabering people. Perfectly timed, the instructor said aloud, "It's okay that your mind wanders. In yoga, we expect it to wander. But whenever it does, just return to your deep breathing." I inhaled and exhaled, trying to stay with my breath.

Then, I imagined Darth Vader laughing in the background.

After many minutes that felt like hours, I found myself with my face smashed against the mat, butt raised up in the air, arms threaded between each other, and sweat pouring all over my body. For a brief moment, I actually felt a sense of relief. This had to be the most rigorous exercise I had ever done. Then the giant man next to me expelled a very audible fart, and I lost all sense of spiritual connection. While I was contorted, I rolled my eyes over to Torrin and could see him laughing with his face smashed into the mat.

I couldn't hold back. I started laughing hysterically and put my arm over my face to try to conceal my immaturity. I grabbed my shirt, which I had taken off long ago, and buried my face in what had to be the most hilarious and shameful moment of my life. Trying to hide behind every fiber of my clothing, the teacher noticed what was happening, and announced, "Let it be known that everything that happens in here is a natural element of our existence. Labored breathing, expelled gas, sweaty bodies, that's all part of what makes us so uniquely alive."

For a moment, my laughter stopped because the instructor made some sense. Then, right on cue, Torrin ripped a fart that was even louder than the big man next to me. I lost it. He lost it. We were both crying of laughter, and everyone turned their head toward us. The instructor walked over to us and asked if we needed a moment outside of the room to recollect. We straightened up our faces, assured her that we were okay, and told her we wouldn't let it happen again. As she slowly walked away, Torrin turned toward me and whispered, "What? Don't look at me like that. I was just expelling gas and being uniquely alive, like she said." He quietly laughed, and I quietly shook my head at him.

With the laughter under control, I continued to try the poses. Arms shaky and legs wobbly, I finished out the last few poses and pleaded in my mind for it to be over. Just as I thought I couldn't take anymore, the instructor called out, "The time has come for Savasana. Gently find your way to your back and roll down vertebrae by vertebrae. Shake out your arms and legs, and let them fall naturally to the floor. Take up as much space as you need here. For those of you who are new to yoga, this is perhaps one of the most important poses because it allows the body and mind to rest together as one." I was on the floor, nearly passed out, with sweat pouring down my face and body. Bodies lined the ground like the aftermath of a massacre, breathing heavily and sweating profusely. Scents of body odor and lavender swirled in the air and created a unique mixture of serenity and sacrifice. The only light in the room came from the faint flicker of candle flames.

Trying to get comfortable, I lay my arms and legs out. Just as my left arm touched the floor, I felt a slimy, warm sensation and looked over to find that the large man had accidentally laid his hand on mine. He immediately snapped it back and turned away from me, embarrassed. I wiped my hand off and tried to get my mind off how gross it was. As we lay there in silence, I felt my mind running a million miles a minute. Despite the peaceful live piano in the background, and the sound of slow breathing all around me, I kept thinking about anything and everything. Thoughts about what I was going to eat afterward, not being able to decide between a steak sandwich or chicken strips. Thoughts about how weird the whole experience had been. Thoughts about the instructor and how she became a yoga teacher. Thoughts about being on an island somewhere and relaxing by crystal blue water. But amongst all these thoughts, I felt a sense of relaxation like never before. I continued to enjoy the silence, the relaxation, and the slowing of the mental treadmill as I waited for the session to end.

"Gently wiggle your fingers and toes," the instructor was back, "When you're ready, start to flutter your eyes open." The corpses all came to life. Bodies slowly moved and shifted. Sitting up, the instructor closed with some inspirational words, "In yoga, we are one. The trees, the sun, the flowers, and the seas, your friends, your loved ones, and even your enemies, we are all one. Thank you, friends, for joining me in class tonight. Namaste." As I bowed, all I could think about was how thankful I was to have said, "Yes," to Nate's text message. Then, as I rolled up my yoga mat, I thought about how first dates, marriage proposals, jobs, promotions, friendships, negotiations, social change, and even the beginning of a yoga practice are all a result of one word. As it turns out, some of the best things in life happen after the word, "Yes."

The Science Behind
Saying "Yes!"

T here are 171,476 words in the English dictionary[1]. But, it only takes one to change the rest of our lives. One word can take us to the tops of the highest mountains or the depths of the deepest oceans. It can get us to jump out of perfectly good airplanes or start new, revolutionary businesses. It can even help us fall in love. In the years that have passed since my "Yoga on the Bluff" experience, I have regularly practiced yoga anywhere from three to five times a week, voluntarily instructed a few classes of my own, and even joined a few yoga-based retreats. It has taken me from Joshua Tree to San Francisco, brought me everlasting friendships, encouraged me to conduct research studies about yoga and communication at San Diego State University, and pushed me to shift my perspective on the health of my mind, body, and spirit. So, how did I go from hating the idea of yoga to completely falling in love with it? The answer is simple. I said, "Yes," to something that I initially wanted to say, "No," to. Many times in life we are presented with concealed opportunities that we pass along because saying, "No," is easy, familiar, and most of all, comfortable. The word, "No," is typically a fear-response, most useful in situations of genuine danger[2]. On the other hand, "Yes," is an *Opportunistic Word.* "Yes," can lead to new places, new friends, new hobbies, new jobs, new lovers, new ideas, and best of all, new experiences.

I have witnessed first-hand how one word can drastically alter people's lives. As a professor, I have implemented a "Yes" comfort challenge as a form of homework for personal development. Students from all ages have participated, including as young as 16 years old and as old as 62 years old. After reading through over 1,000 reflections, there was one overarching theme that emerged: Students felt like their lives drastically improved after challenging themselves. For example, Brian Applegate was a happy-go-lucky, young student who loved action sports - skateboarding, surfing, and swimming through caves in La Jolla. Before I met him, he had the fun idea to build his own skateboard. While taking it on a test run, Brian got into an accident that left him in a coma for five weeks. When he finally woke up, he was delusional, confused, and felt disconnected from his own identity. As time passed, he became depressed. He pushed away his family, friends, and coworkers. He became discouraged from going to school. The word, "No," circled in his mind. He didn't want to do anything that seemed uncomfortable, unfamiliar, or uncertain. Then, I had the amazing privilege of having Brian as a student shortly after his accident. We worked together throughout the semester using various, small comfort challenges, most of which involved saying, "Yes," more often. In just sixteen weeks, Brian's attitude about life completely changed. He opened up to his family and friends again. If you met him now, he'd be smiling from ear-to-ear, and he'd probably ask you to go on an adventure with him[3].

Another student, Jack, who served in the military for over 20 years, was having a difficult time adjusting to civilian life. Jack was the kind of student who sat in the last row at the back of the classroom, constantly checking the door and scanning the room to make sure the area was safe and secure. He was unable to be close with his wife, children, or friends, and spent most of his time alone at home. I remember at the beginning of the semester he told me that he wasn't sure if he'd ever be happy again. But, as our semester progressed and Jack engaged in several comfort challenges, everything started to change. He tried sitting in the front row of the classroom, he engaged in conversations with younger students, and by the end of the course, he hosted his very own barbecue for all of his close friends and family. For Jack, it was the first time he was able to freely socialize with his favorite people since retiring from the service. I'll never forget the smile on his face when he told me that story.

As one more example, I had a student who had a terrible phobia of heights. Sasha was a single mother of two children and spent the past 40 years of her life avoiding anything related to heights. She couldn't even step up onto a curb without feeling a jolt of discomfort.

Sasha and I worked together all semester to help her overcome this phobia. The challenges included stepping up onto a high curb, then onto a bench, then onto a table. After just ten challenges, she did something that absolutely blew my mind. She jumped out of a plane! Her entire life she had dreamed of skydiving, but thought it would never be possible because of her fear of heights. But, throughout our course, she learned that fear is just a manipulative emotion that holds us back from living the life we want to live. In order to cross free-falling off her bucket list, she had to say, "Yes," to the discomfort. And, it was at 10,000 feet in the sky that Sasha discovered a newfound comfort in one of the most unusual places.

The fascinating part is there's science to back all of these stories up. Most of us have heard of the *Butterfly Effect*, which is the idea that a butterfly flaps its wings on one side of the world and over time, weather patterns start to shift. Soon enough, it builds and swirls until a tornado forms on other side of the world[4]. However, most people don't know that it is built on research, which scientists refer to as *Chaos Theory*. The idea is that one small thing happens, which leads to other small things happening, and it keeps going and going without an end[5]. The result is that infinite possibilities can occur and it removes predictability from the equation[6]. For me, the simple act of trying out yoga completely changed my life. As a result of saying, "Yes," that one time to my friend's invite, I have traveled to new places, met new people, tried new activities, and best of all, developed a deeper sense of spirituality and connection to all that surrounds me. After all, "It is only when we dare to act in new ways that a change can actually be said to occur"[7]. When we practice openness in our environment, both mentally and emotionally, we expand our brain's ability to process *Peripheral Information*, which is information happening outside of our central line of focus[8]. In simpler words, when we say, "Yes," and open ourselves up to the unknown, we will experience a life beyond what we thought was possible. Our line of sight expands, our capacity for learning grows, and our perception of possibility magnifies.

Language is more powerful than most people realize. The words we choose in our everyday conversations shape the reality we live in. For example, if you walked up to a stranger who was walking a dog right now, and said, "*You* are amazing," they'd probably give you a sneering eye, a turned-up nose, or a look of confusion. However, if you approached and said, "*Puppies* are amazing," they'd probably smile and engage in the shared love. One word can change everything. Taking this one step further, there is a theory known as *Emotional Granularity*, which is the idea that our ability to accurately describe our emotions, with the right words, has a significant effect on our ability to cope with everyday life[9]. For instance, if I'm a little bored and unmotivated, I might say that I'm feeling *lethargic*. If, instead, I said that I was *depressed*, research suggests that I would actually start to feel the true symptoms of depression. Again, the words we choose in our everyday language have a huge impact on how we live our lives!

This idea is so powerful that big companies are taking advantage of this language-driven revolution. The power of the word, "Yes," has become a staple in the culture of wildly successful companies including Google, Apple, Virgin, the Ritz Carlton, and an award-winning restaurant – Ocean Prime. Google, for example, celebrates its "Culture of Yes" and credits some of their most ground-breaking work – including self-driving cars and off-shore, wind-power grids, to their encouragement of using "Yes" more often[10]. Virgin Hotels redesigned guests' phones to only feature one button that says, "YES!" in giant, red letters at the center of the phone. When the CEO was asked about this decision, he explained it as motivation for the employees to find ways to say, "Yes," to more requests, and as a message to hotel guests that no matter their question or need, the service staff will find a way to help[11]. Similarly, Ocean Prime has won awards and been famously touted for its impeccable service. Their secret? They follow one important motto at their restaurant: "The answer is, 'Yes.' What is the question?"[12]. By utilizing this mindset, employees are able to treat guests like royalty, which increases customer satisfaction and retention.

I actually had a chance to experience a 'Culture of Yes' first-hand when I worked for one of the largest tech companies in the world (to avoid a conflict of interest, I'm not allowed to say the name of the company, but if you think of a fruit, it might help). In relation to customer service, we were encouraged to never use the word, "No," and to instead always figure out a way to convert it to a "Yes." For example, if a customer had a question that I didn't know the answer to, instead of saying, "I don't know," or "no," I might try something like, "Whoa, great question. Let's find out together." Then we'd use our resources to exchange the limitation into a possibility. There's a valuable lesson here. Not only can saying the word, "Yes," help us create better customer interactions, it can also help create more human connection. The word "No" is a divisive word. It creates a barrier between us and other people. It can even be thought of as a word of rejection[13].

It should be noted that the goal of this section is not to simply say, "Yes," to everything. That would eliminate our ability to be authentic, of course. If you've ever seen the show, *The Office*, then you're probably familiar with Andy Bernard. He's the epitome of a 'yes man' – in some instances he will completely agree with the boss, then turn right around and agree with one of his coworkers who disagrees with the boss. Similarly, in the movie, *Yes Man*, Jim Carrey's character ends up doing some pretty wild things, like sleeping with an elderly woman and fighting while drunk at a bar. So, we don't want to be like these people-pleasers, which means we don't want to just say, "Yes," to everything (in fact, some of us might benefit from learning how to say, "No," more often). For instance, if we say, "Yes," to every additional project that people ask us to participate in, we might soon have a plate that is too full for our working appetite.

Likewise, we also want to avoid saying, "No," to everything. Instead, we are looking at slowing down our automatic decision-making process, which typically involves uncertainty avoidance, face-saving, and defense mechanisms[14]. By default, we tend to respond in ways that keep us within our comfort zone. Based on a theory called the *Positive-Negative Asymmetry Effect*, negativity is often more likely to influence our decisions than positivity[15]. On one hand, this is a great skill to have as a human. It has helped us evolve and adapt over centuries. For example, a snake bite can be deadly, so when we see a snake, we immediately and automatically retreat. But for situations that aren't life or death, like attending a social event, we still tend to have the same defense mechanisms show up. This is an issue because we are limiting ourselves from reaching our highest potential. According to the New York Times, "the problem with,

'No' as a starting place is that it polarizes, prompts defensiveness and shuts down innovation, collaboration and connection"[2].

This section is dedicated to freeing us from our attraction toward comfort, and to instead challenge us to explore discomfort. To be clear, it is not encouraged to say, "Yes," to things that are dangerous, illegal, or downright immoral. The goal is to develop more inner confidence, more authenticity with the choices we make, and to eventually strengthen the influence of positivity over negativity on our decisions. Ultimately, we are looking to slow down when making choices. That way, we can respond freely, intentionally, and authentically. So, the next time you think about the 171, 476 words that you can use when deciding whether or not to do something, think about the one that just might change everything: Because you never know where the magic might happen.

Comfort Challenge 4: Say Yes!

As you travel through the next couple days, look for an opportunity to say, "Yes," to something you feel inclined to say, "No," to. (Obviously, if it is dangerous or challenges your morality/religion/spirituality/etc., then keep it a "No!") Whether it is a new activity, a hobby, a favor, a request, or anything in between, be sure to stay mindful through the experience and try to stay present with what it actually feels like to do something different for a change. There's a good chance you will feel hesitant or uncomfortable at first, but stick with it. Have some fun, try something new, and see what happens!

5

Buddha's Hideout

Like most people at some point in their 20s, I was on a mission to 'find myself.' At first, I wasn't really too sure where to look. I checked under my bookshelf and didn't see myself there. I looked behind my cabinets and in my dresser, but I wasn't there either. I traveled to Iceland; nope not there. I went to Switzerland, Germany, France, Spain, Mexico, and the Czech Republic... I couldn't find myself anywhere! I decided the next course of action was to start trying new exercises and hobbies to find myself a passion. I stumbled upon a website called Meetup.com and a whole new slew of crazy experiences began.

To give a glimpse of some of the interesting and unusual things I participated in... I went to an "energy" play-shop in a local karate studio where we tried to conjure up our fire and ice energy and transmit it into other people. One time, I ended up at a College Olympics event where there were over 150 people competing and playing games. It wasn't until I showed up that I realized it was a *drinking* Olympics. There was only one problem: I didn't drink alcohol back then. Another time I ended up at a fitness camp where we ran around, sang songs, and played games that I haven't played since elementary school, all while trying to be sold a nutritional supplement.

One other time I had to walk out from a meetup that was even too wild for me.

While I was working for a week up in San Francisco, I was recommended to check out a meetup where people increase vitality through connection. Little did I know, they meant sexual vitality. When I arrived, I opened the door and saw a sign that read, "Orgasmic Meditation Meetup, Come See What Life is Like Powered by Orgasms." I quickly looked around and saw that all the attendees were dressed in various color shirts that said in big print on the front, "Powered by Orgasms." Several of them had their eyes closed and were making soft moaning sounds. One person sounded like they were climaxing. Naturally, I turned around and left as quickly as I could.

But it got me thinking. While I wasn't ready for orgasmic meditation, maybe I should at least try out this meditation stuff that was getting popular. I had recently heard that big businesses like Google and Apple were implementing mindfulness and meditation as a way to improve the lives of their employees. I figured, what better place to look for myself than inward? Maybe if there was a meetup where I could give a basic breathing session a shot, that might be kind of cool.

A couple weeks after the San Francisco trip, I mustered up the courage to search for a meditation meetup in San Diego. After skipping several groups because they had cultish names like, "Mastering Meditation: The Power is Within You" or "Stop Medicating, Start Meditation to Save Your Life," I finally found one that met in Ocean Beach named "Buddha's Hideout." It had a pretty cool name and the description was pretty friendly. I figured that at least if it was lame or weird, I could just leave to go to the beach.

I made the 20-minute drive to the location, followed my GPS, and ended up at an old office building. The place was ancient. The windows out front were all tinted black and there were cobwebs strung about. I entered the first door which lead to a narrow staircase. Once I made it to the second floor, there were several doors to choose from. The carpet beneath me was stained and terribly ugly. The hallway smelled musty and ancient. I started to get a little nervous, but kept walking. Room 203... Room 204... Looking for 210.... Room 208, and finally the last door at the end of the hall – Room 210. I gently opened the solid wood door and made my way inside. This is when things got a little strange.

"Welcome to dharma, my good friend," the man in the center said as I walked in. The room was silent. "Come on in, take your shoes off and place them right over there. If you need, you can borrow a cushion from that box in the corner. Then, just get comfortable. We're practicing our first Samadhi and working on setting our mantras." "Okay," I replied a bit awkwardly, having no idea what he was talking about.

I looked around and realized that we were inside a converted office space. There were computers and desks around the room, several clocks from different time zones on the walls, and an antique time-clock for punching in and punching out. The room smelled like the inside of an old, unused camper van. The air was musty and stagnant, which didn't seem very enlightening to me. I thought to myself, "If I was Buddha, I definitely would not hide out here."

All kinds of different people were seated throughout the room. One guy was wearing oversized, white cloth pants and no shirt. Another guy was wearing yoga pants and a tank top with a lotus flower printed on the front. One girl had a tight-fitted, black tank-top and massive, balloon-type brown pants that flowed all over the floor. And the leader, who went by the name of Roshi, was wearing full, orange Tibetan robes, or at least I think that's what they're called. I immediately felt out of place in my dark-blue jeans, pair of flip-flops, and Hawaiian shirt.

I grabbed a cushion and squeezed myself between the guy with the yoga pants and the girl with the balloon pants. I realized they were dressed that way because they wanted to be comfortable while sitting still for long periods of time. I gazed down at my stiff, blue jeans and realized they were definitely not as good of an option. They both had their eyes closed, legs crossed, and hands on their knees, making little rings with their thumbs and index fingers. I looked at them and tried to match the way they were sitting. I crossed one leg over the other, then practiced touching my thumb to my different fingers.

While I was trying to get comfortable in this most unusual place, Roshi put on an atmospheric soundtrack of whooshes and waves, then announced, "My friends, the journey to enlightenment begins here and now. The power of group meditation is much more powerful than meditating alone, so if you feel lots of energy flowing through you, that is natural and expected. Let the dharma take over. I will be setting a timer for 20 minutes, and once we have made it, we will end with a Tibetan singing-bowl sound bath. We will begin with a chant in the sound of Om. Okay friends, let's go." Yet again, I had no idea what he was saying. Everyone else in the room closed their eyes and started humming an Om sound. But, I stayed quiet and kept my eyes open for a moment. It was such a strange sight to see. Everyone was sitting almost identically and making weird movements with their mouth as they chanted. I thought about getting up and running to the beach, but it'd be terribly awkward to leave at this point. Finally, I closed my eyes and tried to join in. After a few seconds, I felt nervous and peeped one eye open to see if maybe they were trying to play a joke on me. Nope, everyone was still right where they were, eyes closed, and humming. So, I closed my eyes again and tried to join in. After about a minute of chanting, Roshi announced that it was time for silent meditation.

Naturally, I couldn't stop thinking. I was thinking about how weird it was, how strange everyone in the room was, how bizarre Roshi was, and of course, how crazy I was for signing up. I was thinking about how I would have rather been at the beach, or anywhere else for that matter. I thought about what I should do the next day. I thought about how uncomfortable my body felt. But, after a couple minutes of all this noise, something changed. I'm pretty sure I fell asleep and started dreaming, but here's what happened.

With my eyes closed, I started to see galaxies of stars. Endless galaxies of distant space. It was stunningly beautiful. The backdrop was black and there were sparkling purple and white speckles sprinkled throughout. It looked like colorful dust that was being illuminated by hidden lights. Suddenly, a giant object appeared at the center of the galaxy. It was a great big can of Dr. Pepper. It zoomed in from the center and circled around like it was on display at an art museum. It became huge. Big enough to share with giants. Then it faded quickly and a McDonald's bag appeared. As the bag got closer, a Big Mac and handful of fries floated out of the top. In a matter of seconds, they sunk back into the bag and it went away. Then, a Wendy's Frostee showed up. The spoon inside it was made of gold and looked heavier than the sword in the stone. It went on like this for the next 20 minutes with various unhealthy foods popping up at the center of the galaxy in my mind. I thought I was tripping from some kind of second-hand laced incense. Finally, I was awakened by the singing bowl, which was incredibly loud for its size. Roshi gently spoke to bring us all out of our trance, "Welcome back my friends. Let's talk about our journey." We spent the next 30 minutes talking about how Buddha exists in the flapping of a butterfly's wings, and how Dharma is all around us.

It's in our car, it waits for us at home, it's there when we wake up and still there when we sleep. I couldn't help but think that Dharma sounded pretty damn similar to Santa Claus.

Confused about my experience with a galaxy of junk food, I spoke with Roshi at the end of the meetup. He looked at me with a scrunched-up face, and his first response was, "Hmm, did you eat any pork today?" I wasn't sure what that had to do with anything, so I said, "Nope, no pork." He stared at the ground and scratched his head. "How about meat, have you eaten any animal products in the past 24 hours?" "Well, I had a chicken sandwich for lunch today and steak for dinner last night." He stepped back and looked appalled. "There you have it. Your collective subconscious was punishing you for your mistreatment of animals." "Really?" I replied, "Well what am I supposed to eat then?" He opened his hands in a welcoming gesture and said, "Plants, of course." I half-smirked and coyly responded, "But then wouldn't I be punished for my mistreatment of plants?" He suggested that I should leave since I wasn't going to take spirituality seriously.

*   *   *

I have to admit, despite having weird visualizations of space, I really enjoyed how peaceful and relaxing it was to take some time to sit still. While this specific experience was very uncomfortable and completely out of the ordinary, it gave me enough courage to try meditation in various capacities over the next few months. After having many interesting and bizarre experiences, I found an app for my phone that has guided audio meditation specifically made for everyday, modern people[1]. No spirituality attached, no baggage, no rules, just a relaxing voice that helps me stay focused on my breath. It has helped me lessen my anxiety, increase my focus and productivity, improve my relationships, and gain an overall sense of balance in life. I would have never taken the steps toward such a healthy mind if it wasn't for challenging my comfort up in that old, dusty business office. So, even though I didn't find Buddha hiding up in that dusty, old business complex that night, it's safe to say that I found something equally magnificent. I found myself.

The Science Behind
Mini-Vacations

I magine being able to take a pill that makes you feel more relaxed, takes away stress, improves your relationships, makes you more aware of yourself and your surroundings, and makes everyday life seem lighter, more peaceful, and more rewarding. It's free, you can take it anywhere, anytime, and it's completely legal. On top of that, there are absolutely no side effects. Would you take it?

While this might sound like the plot for the popular movie, *Limitless*, there is actually something we can do each day that can help us in so many ways and does not involve any pills. The best part is that it is completely free, absolutely simple, and available to us all. It's called *Mindfulness Meditation,* which is the act of sitting quietly, focusing on the breath, and paying attention to the current moment. Personally, I like to think of it as a *Mini-Vacation*. While most of us plan some time off during the year (which is typically much earned and much needed), not enough of us carve time out for ourselves during each day. The benefits of mini-vacations with mindfulness meditation are extraordinary. We can reduce our anxiety, depression, and stress, and feel a greater sense of compassion, gratitude, and empathy[2,3,4,5,6].

Imagine that you are the CEO of a startup company. You're standing at a glass door, waiting to meet with corporate executives from all over the world, hoping to gain millions of dollars in investments. If your pitch works well, your company could become globally recognized, your product could become wildly popular, and you could create jobs for hundreds, if not thousands of people. However, if you screw up, all of your hard work could go to waste, your startup could go bankrupt, and you could become recognized as a business failure from here on out. It's up to you to

create an incredible impression and make the sale.
Three... two... one. You open the door.

It is inevitable that business can incorporate some
high-level, intense situations. Whether it's an
investment pitch, a stakeholder meeting, a job
interview, or a merger, it has become increasingly
important that employees become more mentally
resilient and stable in the workplace. That's why
companies like Google, Target, and General Mills,
among many others these days, are all utilizing
meditation and mindfulness to reduce workplace
stress, increase work-life balance, and improve
employee satisfaction[7]. In fact, mindfulness is now so
affluent in business that it has become its very own
billion-dollar business[8]. With mindfulness-training
companies like Search Inside Yourself (started by
Google) and The Mindsight Institute (started by best-
selling author and neurobiologist, Dr. Dan Siegel), it's
becoming more difficult to ignore the positive benefits
of taking care of your mind. Not only has meditation
made a big impact in big business, it has also found its
way into the military as well.

Snipers use it to steady their aim, Navy Seals use it
for high-pressure situations, and Royal Marine trainees

are using it to prepare for combat. They call it *Mindfulness-Based Mind Fitness Training*, or *M-Fit* for short[9]. When asked about the inclusion of meditation, Jeffrey Bearor, who oversees Marine Corps training, said in an NBC news article, "This is about mental preparation to better handle stress"[10]. Further along in the article, Bearor brings up the fact that they have lots of help for Marines after extremely stressful situations, like counselors, physicians, and mental health specialists, but they are using meditation as a proactive tool that prepares soldiers to deal with intense scenarios *before* they even happen. One general justifies meditation by referring to it as "pushups for the brain"[10]. Maybe it's just me, but I like to imagine that in the future there will be sergeants yelling at combat trainees, "Drop and give me 20... brain pushups!" They won't be the only ones engaging in brain workouts, since there's another group of elite people who have started touting the benefits of mindfulness: athletes.

Imagine you are standing on the edge of a diving board over three stories high, the wind is gusting, and millions of people are watching you. If you pull off the flips you've been practicing, the whole world will admire and love you. However, if you mess up, there is a chance you will become a disgrace, and the world will bow their heads in disappointment. Three... two... one. You jump.

Similar to the business pitch scenario mentioned earlier, being in a situation where the world is watching would be pretty intense. As with any Olympic event, athletes are put in high-pressure situations that require incredible physical abilities. But, there's another piece to the performance puzzle that often gets overlooked: the mind. As a result of trial and research, Olympic athletes have started incorporating meditation as a method to perform at an even higher level. During an interview with the Huffington Post, Shannon Miller, a gold-medalist in gymnastics, said, "In the Olympic games, everyone is talented. Everyone trains hard. Everyone does the work. What separates the gold medalists from the silver medalists is simply the mental game"[11]. Similarly, Jamie Anderson, who took the gold medal for snowboarding slopestyle, said that staying "chilled-out" during competition was her secret to success[11]. How she does it? Meditation and yoga. Not only are Olympic athletes sitting down and taking breaths, top-performers from a range of sports are participating as well. Kobe Bryant, Tiger Woods,

LeBron James, Michael Jordan, and even the Seattle Seahawks practice meditation to improve their minds, and, ultimately, improve their game[11,12]. In order to better relate to emotions, thoughts, and feelings as they arise, especially in times of difficult situations, people are in need of a learnable skill that helps them maintain a calm, clear, and peaceful approach to those internal processes. Meditation, or a 'mini-vacation for the mind,' is just that skill.

So, how does meditation, an exercise that is all about sitting still, closing your eyes, and taking some deep breaths, fit in with the theme of stepping out of our comfort zones? Well, if you haven't tried it yet, it's actually pretty difficult to sit still for a prolonged amount of time while doing absolutely nothing. We're so used to a fast-paced society that moves in fast-forward, always checking phones and computers, running to and from the office or class, rushing to the gym, and barely sleeping a wink at night. It can be surprisingly uncomfortable to power down, unplug, and switch off. But, once again, that's exactly why we're here: to become more comfortable with being uncomfortable.

The good news is that your experience does not have to be as wild as mine. You won't need to go to a meditation meetup in a dusty, old office "dojo." While there are many different approaches to meditation, for our purposes, we are just going to think of it as taking some time out for ourselves. If you find that it really helps and you enjoy it, there are many resources for continuing the journey and developing a deeper practice. My personal favorite is an app called *Headspace,* because they make it friendly, fun, and accessible for everyone[1].

In essence, meditation can help just about anyone gain a greater sense of focus, relaxation, and clarity. Whether you might be going into big business, joining the military, participating in the Olympics, or doing any number of other possibilities, by taking care of the mind we can become more accepting, more grateful, more resilient, more aware, and less judgmental[13]. Also, by better taking care of our own minds, we can take better care of others around us, which strengthens our relationships.

So, imagine being able to do something that makes you feel more relaxed, takes away stress, improves your relationships, makes you more aware of yourself and everything around you, and makes everyday life seem lighter, more peaceful, and more rewarding. It's free, you can do it anywhere, anytime, and it's completely legal. The best part is that you don't need a plane, train, car, or shuttle to get there. There's no heavy suitcases to lug around, no cooler to pack, no lay-overs, no traffic, no sunburns, and no travel agency to consult. It's as easy as closing your eyes and taking a few breaths. You now have a handful of round-trip tickets to your very own Mini-Vacation destination with mindfulness meditation. Congratulations, you've earned it!

Comfort Challenge 5: Mini-Vacation

For this comfort challenge, the idea is that you carve just a little bit of time out for yourself from all the distractions, deadlines, and duties of everyday life, just like a mini-vacation from the day. Find a quiet place, get comfortable, and set a timer for 5, 10, 15, or 20 minutes depending on how you're feeling. If it's your very first time, I recommend just three to five minutes to test it out. Then, just kick back, close your eyes, and relax. Enjoy a bit of time to do absolutely nothing. If you can't stop thinking, just focus on what it feels like to breathe. Inhale for four seconds, hold full for four seconds, exhale for four seconds, and hold empty for four seconds. Note: You can replace four with any number! Once your timer goes off, take a deep breath, stretch, and keep going about your day. Repeat as needed.

6

Swimming with Glaciers

"So, you're telling me... all I have to do is jump in some cold water to get an all-you-can-eat pancake breakfast for free?" My traveling companion, Erika, nodded and smiled, "Yep. My friend is the owner of the next hostel we're staying at. She agreed that if you jump in the glacier lagoon, you can have as many pancakes as your heart desires!" I nodded, understood that this was a no brainer, and clenched my teeth, "Hell yeah. I'm in."

And thus, we return to the beautiful, natural playground of Iceland for this story. Where volcanos are on the brink of eruption, mountains stand as reminders of the Vikings that once lived there, the sky ignites in a glorious swirl of colors known as the Northern Lights, and the elderly locals believe that doing a daily cold-water swim each morning will prolong your life. No joke, one morning while staying at a hostel during a freezing snow-storm, I saw a sight I couldn't believe. Two older women, about the age of seventy or eighty, were wearing one-piece swimsuits and walking toward the nearby cove of water. Without hesitation, they dove in and began swimming.

I thought to myself that these old ladies were absolutely nuts. It would take some serious bartering for me to do something like that. Hell, I'd have a hard time even turning my hot shower into a lukewarm shower. Little did I know, a free stack of pancakes was all it would take.

After the snow-storm passed and we were able to leave the artistic town of Seyðisfjörður (say-dis-fure-dur), Erika and I made our way down the Eastern coastal part of the "Ring Road," which is a narrow highway that travels around the entire country. Thankfully, after our near-death experience in the highlands, we didn't have any more car troubles. We did, however, pass by all sorts of unbelievable sights. There were wild horses, playful reindeer, volcanic rock piles, steamy geysers, public swimming holes, giant craters, and majestic waterfalls. At one point, there was even a road sign that had an illustration of a dragon, and in big block letters it said, "Beware of Sea Monsters." This place was a real testament to surreal nature.

As we neared a one-lane bridge, I looked off in the distance and saw a giant stream of water coming from the mountains all the way to the ocean. Sticking up out of the stream, like giant boulders, were huge pieces of blue ice that made the entire scene quite shivery. The stream was known as Jökulsárlón, a fancy Icelandic name for Ice Beach.

It was a river of water that came from a melting glacier high up in the nearby mountains and stretched all the way down to the Atlantic Ocean. It was a very popular destination for tourists to take photos and videos of the scenery. Some tourists were even brave enough to step out onto one of the giant, flat pieces of floating ice to take some souvenir snapshots. Other tourists would pay heaps of money to hop in a rugged boat that would take them on a tour through the glacier river. Very rare was it that a tourist would take a plunge and actually jump in.

Almost no one in history (besides the elderly locals, of course) had ever actually jumped in with only swim trunks, swam out to one of the glacier chunks, and back. Except, that's exactly what I did.

As we pulled off the highway in our banged-up, rental Subaru, we parked in a dirt lot where there were typically more cars than parking spots. But, since the season was late Fall and approaching Winter, tourism was less popular at this time of year. The weather was colder, the roads were more dangerous, and the snow was more frequent, which meant less crowds. As we parked, we were the only car in the dirt lot. I checked the temperature and shivered as I read 0 degrees Celsius (32 degrees Fahrenheit), which converts in most people's brains to freezing. "Are you sure you want to do this?" Erika, dressed in a huge wool sweater, a thick scarf, an oversized beanie, and a pair of gloves that would be suitable for ice-fishing, wasn't sure about my idea to go for a little swim. I spoke up, "You're sure I will get free pancakes out of it?" She gaffed, "Yes, Kevin, but I can also buy pancake mix for like a couple Euro, which is like a few dollars." I laughed back, "Yeah, but that's totally different. Then it wouldn't be a free all-you-can-eat pancake breakfast. Besides, how many chances do you get to come to Iceland and swim with glaciers?" She rolled her eyes and sighed, "Okay, but if you end up dying over a stack of pancakes I hope you know I will not be upset."

I stepped out of the car, wrapped a towel around my waist, and stripped off my snow-pants to change into my swim trunks. It felt just like being back in San Diego getting ready to surf, except for the temperature being about 50 degrees colder and the population being about 100% less people. I grabbed a towel out of my backpack - not that I was expecting it to keep me warm - took off my shirt, and walked toward the water. Just before diving in, a very light snowfall started. "Perfect timing," I thought to myself. I slid my hands back and forth against each other and jumped up and down a few times, trying to stay warm. This was one of the moments where I knew I needed just 20 seconds of insane courage to take the plunge. If I waited any longer, I'm positive I would have talked myself out of it.

I threw the towel down on a nearby rock and ran as fast as I could toward the water. As my feet started splashing in the shallow-end, I ignored the painful, icy temperature and dove headfirst into the water. I figured if I just went as fast as I could, I might not notice how cold it was until later. Sort of like those folks in eating competitions who eat 100 hotdogs in less than a minute so their body can't register all the food, I tried to swim as fast as I could, hoping that my body wouldn't register the painfully cold water. My calculations were way off. The water was absolutely freezing. The glacier chunk that I was aiming for was about 500 feet away, which on shore seemed quite doable. Once I was in the water, paddling desperately, it seemed quite impossible.

No matter how fast I tried to flap my arms, I couldn't avoid the cold. My body felt like it was constricting to the point of no return. Like a snake wrapping around every inch of my torso, the cold water was suffocating. I kept my eyes closed and just kept moving forward. My skin was blistering with the sensation of needles stabbing me all over. I immediately decided that no amount of pancakes were worth this torture. My brain started to turn upside down. "Keep pushing!" I told myself. I kept flailing my arms and kicking my feet. I recalled a friendly fish once telling me to 'just keep swimming,' so I did. When I opened my eyes, I immediately realized I was way off course. The current of the flowing water was sweeping me out toward the ocean while I was trying to swim in a straight line. Now, trying to fight the current, as well as fight the cold, I redirected my angle and forcefully continued. Just a few more feet to the damn ice rock. Keep going.

Just when I thought I couldn't make it any further, I opened my eyes and saw that the glacier chunk was just several feet away. I flapped uncontrollably, got ever closer, and managed to tap it with my right hand. Victory! I tried to proclaim my excitement in a shout of glory, but all that I could manage was a mumble. Then I realized the worst of it all. This was not triumph, this was only the halfway marker. I had to swim all the way back now. And I had to do it soon, or else.

Taking a huge breath, I put my feet on the glacier and pushed off back toward the shore. I convinced myself that there was no other choice but to keep moving. Again, I was desperately waving my arms around in an attempt to swim faster. I closed my eyes and tried to grit through the pain. Again, I felt my brain twist and turn. I started to lose sight of where the water began and where the sky ended. I tried to come up for a breath, but instead went down and gulped water into my lungs. Choking, coughing, and on the brink of death, my body went numb and I froze. For a moment, I was unable to move any part of my body. I was going into hypothermic shock. I did everything I could to tell myself to keep moving. My brain fired off every signal it could to my body, but nothing happened. I was drifting... haplessly, helplessly... hopelessly.

Just when I thought I was done for, my body fired back to life. My mind ran on a treadmill that repeated one phrase: keep moving. I regained the ability to swing my arms violently and kick my legs recklessly. About halfway back to land and I was using everything I had to keep myself from drowning. Just keep swimming, just keep moving, just keep going. As I approached the shore and started to make my way out of the water, my feet felt blistered and unable to bear the weight of my body. My skin was purple all over. I limped toward Erika as she cheered for me. I was in a complete state of delirium. I took the towel that she handed me and didn't even use it to dry off. I just wrapped it around my waist and started walking in the direction of the car. I couldn't feel the cold air outside. I couldn't feel the steps I was taking. I couldn't feel much of anything.

As I made my way toward the car, there were a few more visitors that came along. A family of Asian tourists with big cameras and big jackets were giggling and taking photos of me. Without realizing it, I had developed a fan base. They cheered and said in their best English, "Whoa, surfer boy come to Iceland!" Still with my shirt off and only a pair of wet trunks in 32-degree weather, they asked me to take photos with them. Erika begged me to put a jacket on to warm up, but I ignored her and bathed in the icy stardom. I gave big thumbs-ups to the camera and put my arms around the tourists. They were seriously amazed, and I was seriously dazed.

After a few camera clicks and high fives, Erika pulled me by the arm and took me to the car, where she insisted that I dry off and get warm. She started the engine, blasted the heater, and opened the passenger door. "Get in and get yourself warm. I'm not kidding." She watched as I leaned in toward the car, then she turned around so that I could have my privacy for changing. After a couple minutes, she turned back around and found me passed out on the passenger seat. She ran over and shook me until I came back to my senses. "Kevin, Kevin, c'mon you have to get warm!" I crawled inside and curled up on the seat. "If you don't change right now I'm going to change your clothes for you, and believe me, neither of us want that to happen."

She was right. I pulled the towel over me like a blanket and kicked off my wet trunks. A few minutes later, I was fully dressed in long-johns, snow-pants, a long-sleeve thermal, an over-coat, a knitted beanie, a pair of snow gloves, and a pair of snow socks. The car heater was on full-blast and aimed right at me.

...And I was still cold.

Slowly, as my body started to regain circulation and my blood started to move around, I felt some of the most pain I've ever felt. My entire body was pulsing and throbbing. But, as my senses started to return, I suddenly felt awakened. Not only was my body surging, but my brain also felt like it had just been woken up from a twenty-two-year nap. It was energized, supercharged even. No amount of coffee, energy drink, tea, or soda could have kicked me into this high of a gear. I felt my creativity overflowing as I started to think about song ideas for my band back home. It's not that I was depressed or unhappy before I took the plunge, but I felt the greatest sense of joy and relief afterward. I realized in that moment that nature has an extraordinary power for helping humans become recharged. There is something about Earth's elements, like fresh air, cold water, soft dirt, warm fire, and sunlight, that helps us operate at our highest potential.

The next morning, when we walked into the breakfast room of the hostel, everyone was cheering for me. Word had gotten around that I had taken the frozen-water plunge, and the owner of the hostel even came up to me to shake my hand. She said, in very broken English, that she was proud of me, that I was welcome to all the pancakes I wanted, and that she was going to post the story about me on the hostel's Facebook page. So, I made my victorious walk toward the pancake station and helped myself to a heaping stack, complete with butter and real maple syrup. I sat down, took the first bite, and sank into a state of complete bliss. Erika looked at me in disbelief, "Well," she said, "was it worth it?" I entered another forkful of delicious pancake into my mouth, paused to consider the question, smiled, and replied, "Can you get me another stack?"

The Science Behind
a Dose of Nature

T o some people, putting their hands in the dirt, walking around barefoot, jumping in ice-cold water, or just staring up at the clouds sounds like a great time. To others, not so much. As it turns out, American adults spend more time inside their cars than they do outside[1]. In fact, each year there are less Americans hiking, fishing, camping, exploring, or playing in nature[2]. Considering all the extraordinary benefits that can come from spending time outdoors, this is a huge problem. The solution? It's about time we get wild.

Think about this for a second. Why is it that America's biggest metropolitan city, New York, is home to a sprawling park right in the middle of it? In fact, Central Park is even bigger than some small cities in the country! When the state of New York decided to purchase the park, they paid more for it than the United States paid for the entire state of Alaska back in 1867[3]. When digging up the history on this iconic park, it turns out the reason it was purchased was to "improve public health and contribute greatly to the formation of a civil society"[4].

With this in mind, I decided to go on a tour of the nation to find out whether or not there's nature in the middle of every major city. Since I don't own a plane, a ship, or a lot of money, I used Google Maps and the flight controls of my computer. What I found blew my mind. Every major city had a sprawling urban park right in the middle of it. Aside from the massive Central Park in New York, there's Fairmount Park in Philadelphia (9,200 acres[5]), Griffith Park in Los Angeles (4,310 acres[6]), Presidio Park in San Francisco (1,491 acres[7]), Lincoln Park in Chicago (1,208 acres[8]), and Balboa Park in San Diego (1,200 acres[9]). Regardless of how much we build our infrastructure with skyscrapers and high-rises, our species has continuously included nature as part of the process.

Parks are not merely limited to major cities. Even the buildings within the cities are starting to incorporate trees, bushes, grass, and gardens as part of the architecture, which professionals call *Skyrise Greenery*. Architects are literally drafting the inclusion of living organisms into the blueprints of city buildings[10]. The advent of sky-rise greenery teaches us that nature and business go hand-in-hand. The greenery creates a necessary balance between stress and relaxation that leads to happier, more productive workers[11]. This is not just true at workplaces; it is also happening at housing communities, schools, and shopping malls.

No joke, my girlfriend and I just went on an evening stroll at our nearby mall and stumbled upon a brand-new trend: mini landscapes and terrariums planted on the top of trash cans. Not only were there succulents sprouting up above garbage, there were also potted plants, vertical shrubs that clung to the side of storefronts, and trees all throughout the walkways. Even in a place that is specifically designed for the purchase of clothes and toys, nature has been placed right in the middle of it. Why? Well, researchers dug their hands into this topic and found that greenery in a retail environment can improve people's moods and can even encourage people to spend more money because of the positive feelings associated with mixed vegetation[12]. So, it's pretty obvious that nature is good for us. But what happens to our brain when we play and explore in natural settings?

A simple google search of "how nature affects our brain" pulls up scientific studies from Berkeley University, Stanford University, Washington University, National Geographic, and the New York Times on the positive benefits of nature. Specifically, spending time in nature improves focus, energy, and heart-rate variability, and lowers mental distress, depression, anxiety, heart disease, and migraines[1,13]. In one case study, David Strayer, a cognitive psychologist and outdoor teacher, took several students out to the wilderness, strapped them up to some brain measuring devices, and discovered a performance increase of 50% on creativity and problem-solving tasks after three days[1]. With increased creativity and improved problem-solving skills, it's only a matter of time until we start to gain more confidence and courage in our daily life. Perhaps that's why more and more companies are turning toward nature-based programs and retreats to help with team-building, leadership, confidence, communication, and productivity.

In fact, I run a company in San Diego called The Adventure Learning Project. We have successfully led trips with San Diego State University students, and Coldwell Banker real estate groups, ultimately creating extraordinary bonds through unforgettable adventures. The feedback has been tremendous: "I never realized nature could be so powerful," "I feel like I have a more profound sense of focus on the things in front of me," and "I'm more inspired than ever, my eyes have been opened to a new world of possibility." My company is not the only organization that believes nature can drastically alter the way business is handled. There's also National Outdoor Leadership School, Outward Bound, Kinetic Team Building, and Adventure Associates, to name a few. Clearly, nature is powerful.

Nature is so damn powerful that a view of natural scenery can help alleviate stress, while a television screen with a nature video, or a blank wall, have the same insignificant effect on reducing stress[14]. As part of a research project, participants were asked to accomplish tasks on a computer in a small office. The only difference between participants was that some had a view of nature, some had a television screen showing an image of nature, and some had a blank wall. The results were stunning. There's little-to-no difference between staring at a blank wall and watching nature on television, in regard to lowering stress. People who had the view of nature outside, on the other hand, experienced significantly lower levels of stress. Not only is nature helpful with relieving tension, it is now even being prescribed as a form of medicine. Doctors are actually handing prescription notes to patients, encouraging them to spend some time outdoors. In one clinic alone, their team dished out over 600 prescriptions for nature[15]. The best part is there are no side effects for this type of medicine and it starts working right away.

It only takes as little as 15 minutes in order to start enjoying some of the great benefits that nature has to offer. A team of researchers sent participants on a 15-minute walk in either an urban park or a city area, and discovered that the subjects who were in the park exhibited lower levels of negative emotions and anxiety[16]. Of course, the longer we spend playing and exploring in natural settings, the more benefits we can experience. But, it is helpful to know that in as little as 15 minutes, we can take advantage of going wild.

Nature can do great things for us. It can improve our focus, boost our creativity, and help us have an overall better outlook on life. Naturally, this leads to more inner confidence and courage, which ultimately help us feel more comfortable with being uncomfortable. How you choose to spend your time in nature is completely up to you; whether it's climbing trees, doing some yoga outside, hanging out in a park, stepping into a hot spring, taking a nap beneath some shade, soaking up the sun, smelling some flowers, or hiking up mountains. Regardless of what you choose, know that positive benefits are just around the corner. And to think, that time I swam in the glacial lagoon in Iceland I thought it was just about getting free pancakes and doing something wild for fun. As it turns out, I was getting exactly what the doctor ordered: a full dose of nature.

Comfort Challenge 6: A Dose of Nature

Ready to feel more alive? For this challenge, you're invited to spend at least 15 minutes in nature. Try to make physical contact with natural elements: put your hands in some dirt, touch some leaves, walk barefoot, watch swirling clouds, gaze at twinkling stars, climb some rocks, swim in fresh water, smell a few flowers, or go for a walk outside. The options are infinite and the benefits are endless. Notice the fresh air, the new smells, the beautiful scenery, and how you feel along the way. Let it be relaxing and healing. After all, it's just what the doctor ordered.

7

Lunch with a Monk

When I was in elementary school, we had a contest each year where the winner would get to have lunch with any of their favorite teachers. I didn't win. When I was in high school, we had a competition where the winner would get to have lunch with some high-level business-executives, and most likely get a killer part-time job in the process. I didn't win. When I was in college, they had a special luncheon with some acclaimed professors from other universities for students who won a writing contest. Needless to say, I didn't win that one either. So, when I tell you that many years later, I had a chance to sit down for lunch with my biggest role model, who happens to be an internationally recognized celebrity and founder of a successful company, it might be pretty surprising. How did it happen? A simple thank-you letter.

A few years ago, I was going through a bit of a rough patch. I had just broken up with my girlfriend, and I was going through a slight identity crisis because of graduate school. Laying on my friend's floor while he watched some stand-up comedy on Netflix, I had a panic attack. I cried and rolled around, burying my face in the carpet trying to get out of my own head. Several days later, I was laying at home and feeling pretty depressed. The thought of taking a shower seemed equivalent to boot-camp, and the idea of leaving the house just didn't seem possible. So, I just sat around and watched movies to try to pass the time.

After a few hours of boring movies, I decided that if I was going to wallow, I should at least try to be productive. I typed in "TED Talks" on Google and started watching random episodes about joy, ice-surfing, happiness, cancer, walk-n-talks, and rockets. After each talk, I would scroll and scroll until a title was catchy enough for me to click on it. Then, by some incredibly fortunate chance, I stumbled upon a TED Talk that literally changed my life.

The presenter was an affable and gentle man named Andy. He was a former Buddhist monk and had traveled around the world for 10 years studying meditation. His talk was about taking 10 minutes out of each day to simply sit still and focus on your breath. He claimed that it could reduce depression and anxiety, increase happiness and joy, and improve the overall quality of life. I remember staring at my laptop screen, which was slightly crooked on the end of my bed, knowing that I had found a gem. Fascinated by this man's calm presence and Zen-like nature, I simply had to read more about him.

His name was Andy Puddicombe and he was the co-founder of a company called Headspace, which was a mobile-app designed to help demystify meditation and bring it to the modern public with guided meditations. The app featured specific sessions for kindness, acceptance, appreciation, relationships, anxiety, and creativity. It was an app that could really have a positive impact in anyone's life!

Instantly intrigued, I downloaded Headspace on my somewhat outdated iPhone and gave it a go. During my first sit-down, I listened to Andy's voice guide me through a 10-minute focused-breathing exercise. Having tried meditation in the past (see *Buddha's Hideout*), I was rightfully skeptical about the whole experience. I expected Andy to instruct me to sit a certain way with my legs crossed and twisted, and to chant something along with him. But this was very different from what I expected. He was just a chill guy who lead me through a relaxing breathing exercise.

While Day One wasn't ground-breaking or Earth-shattering, it was incredibly relaxing. I felt a sense of calm afterward. By Day Three, I felt even more calm. On Day Five, I experienced a greater sense of focus, and less rumination in my mind. By Day Eight, something slightly different happened. It was as if the depression had been lifted up, making it feel a little lighter on my shoulders. Feeling this incredible sense of presence and peace, I decided I would commit to a morning meditation practice for the rest of my life (it has been four years and I'm still going strong now). Andy had changed my life.

Thankful beyond belief, I decided to write a letter to Andy. To be honest, I wasn't expecting him to actually read it, or even receive it, but it felt like the right thing to do. I took out a piece of paper from my journal, found a pen, and started to write. Little did I know, the process of spilling out my feelings on paper was really difficult. Trying to be transparent and vulnerable, I felt completely naked and exposed after each sentence. There I was, telling a stranger that he had changed my life, taken me out of depression, lowered my anxiety, and made me a more positive, happy, friendly person. I couldn't get over the idea of him thinking of me as a complete weirdo. Sitting down to write a letter to someone seems so simple and easy, but when I actually went to do it, I felt incredibly uncomfortable.

Pushing through the discomfort, I decided to be completely truthful in the letter. I wrote about having the panic attack, about the depression in my bed, about the feeling of being scared and giving up, and how his TED Talk and app really changed everything. I thanked him for his service to not only me, but to the entire world. I mentioned that if there was ever a possibility for us to partner up on some research, or to sit and have coffee together, I would be interested. And just for the hell of it, I mentioned the idea of swinging by their headquarters and taking a tour of the office, since I didn't live too far away. I signed off with my name and signature, folded up the paper, stuck it in an envelope, and sent it off.

A few days passed and as expected, I didn't hear anything. I kept using the app each morning, and it continued to help me feel more present and less anxious. I remember thinking about how amazing it would be to meet Andy and talk with him in person. What would I even say? What questions would I ask? The idea of it was so exciting.

Then, just a few days later, I received an email notification on my phone. Thinking it was something about work or school, I sluggishly opened the mail app and saw that I had an unread message. It was from someone named Andy, but I figured it was probably just another request for a website change from my grad-school friend named Andrew. I tapped the email and opened it up. I couldn't believe what I was seeing. Right there at the top of the screen it had Andy Puddicombe's name with the Headspace logo next to it. Excited, I started reading the email, "Kevin, I just wanted to say a very big thank you for your kind note.

Are you ever up in the LA area at all? It would be great to meet up. Let me know if you're ever up this way and we can work something out. Very best wishes until then, Andy." I could not believe my eyes. Not only did Andy write back to my letter, he was also interested in having me come up to meet him! This was too good to be true. I wrote back instantly and told him that I would be more than happy to make the drive up to LA from San Diego to meet with him for lunch.

Fast forward a few weeks later, I was cruising up the freeway, blasting some catchy reggae tunes, and rocking out with the windows down. The sun was shining, the wind was refreshingly cool, and I had my favorite Hawaiian shirt on. I was on my way to meet with Andy, and I couldn't have been more excited. I followed the GPS to a location in Venice Beach, where I met him at the Headspace headquarters.

Inside, the office space was beautifully decorated, complete with an outdoor patio, a kitchen, and community work tables. There was a large fountain on the patio that provided an ambient soundtrack of trickling water in the background. The office smelled like a blend of citrus, lavender, and mint, which helped relax my nerves. Just as I imagined, there were no cubicles, and everyone seemed calm and joyful. Andy came out from the studio room, wearing a pair of jeans and a white t-shirt, and greeted me with a smile and friendly hand-shake. "Ready to get a bite?" He asked. I nodded and shook his hand nervously, "Sounds great, Andy." We left the headquarters and walked along Venice Boulevard to a swanky strip of foodie joints. After passing restaurants with clever names like Belly & Snout, The Black Fig, The Carving Board, and Pine & Crane, we ended up at a place named Café Gratitude, which was ironic considering I had never been so grateful for a lunch in my entire life.

As we strolled inside, we were greeted by a young woman at the hostess stand who was dressed like a hippy. She had big flowy pants and a shirt made out of hemp. Her hair was pulled back and she didn't have any make-up on. She walked us to a table, told us she'd be our waitress, and asked if we had eaten at Café Gratitude before. I told her no, so she walked me through a very bizarre ordering process. She smiled and said, "Here at Gratitude, we believe that what we eat is part of who we are. Food isn't something we just put into our bodies; food is something we share an experience with. So, if you look here at the menu," she pointed down at the laminated sheet in front of me, "You'll see that each menu item is an adjective. So, when you're ready to order, you just say 'I am' and then the adjective." I looked at her with a puzzled expression, "Okay, if I were to order this item," I pointed to the word, 'Serene,' which had a description of a mango salad underneath, "then I would just say I am a serene mango salad?" She laughed, "Almost! You only need the adjective. So, you could say, 'I am Serene,' and we would know that you want the mango salad." Chuckling, I responded, "What if I were to just ask for a mango salad?" She smirked, "Well then we wouldn't know what you would want, would we?" I nodded my head and laughed. Andy, also laughing, told me that this was one of his favorite places and I couldn't go wrong with any of the meals. I looked through the options. Deciding on a description of a rice bowl, I looked up and said, "Okay, I'm ready." "Great," the waitress said, "What'll it be?" I smiled and responded, "I am Divine."

As soon as our waitress strolled away, I was too excited to make small talk. Instead, I fired questions off right away. I asked him what it was like to be a monk, why he left London in the first place, what made him continue meditating year after year, and is sex really not allowed for monks. We spoke for about 10 minutes about his journey when I had to pause him. "Wait," I looked at him square in the eyes, "So you're telling me that you spent the better part of 10 years traveling around the world, basically just meditating and not having any sex?" Andy chuckled, "Well, when you put it like that it sounds kinda terrible, but yeah pretty much." I took a sip of the fruit-infused water that was served to me and looked at him again, "Really? None?" He laughed again and said, "None."

The waitress came back over and served us our food. Andy was 'Majestic' and I was 'Divine.' In other words, Andy had ordered a vegan burrito and I ordered a rice bowl. The food was great. Each bite was like a healthy serving of all the nutrition I needed for the week. While we ate, Andy and I shared a great conversation about many things, but one of the most profound things we discussed was the idea of challenging your comfort zone.

I was really interested in finding out what he thought about Comfort Challenges because I really looked up to his advice and insight. He calmly leaned back in his seat, took a sip of his ginger Kombucha, and said with great wisdom, "One of my teachers once told me that the only place where you can learn, grow, explore, discover, and experience what life has to offer, is by stepping out of where you've been." He paused, considered what he just said for a moment, and continued, "I think most of us get along each day feeling like we're doing the same thing over and over. We wake up, brush our teeth, take a shower, make some breakfast, go to work, and so on. It all starts to blur and feel the same." I nodded and smiled in agreement.

He took another sip and continued, "Much like meditation helps us take a step out and become more present with each new moment, I think stepping out of what seems comfortable or familiar sort of forces us into a more mindful state as well. Say you were to wake up tomorrow morning and brush your teeth with your other hand, that would be pretty uncomfortable, wouldn't it? You'd naturally be more present in the moment because you'd have to pay more attention to be able to do it effectively. So, I guess my long-winded answer is that exploring what seems unfamiliar is really the essence of what makes life so rewarding." Nodding along, I agreed, "That's incredible. It's so true what you said about being more mindful in unfamiliar spaces." I got more excited as I spoke, "Like if you were to walk through your front door and make your way to your bedroom with the lights on, that's one thing. But imagine if you tried to do it with the lights out. You'd pay more attention to each step, where the walls are, you'd definitely touch more things along the way, you'd listen closely to any sounds that might give you clues, and so on and so forth." He flashed a big smile, "Exactly."

We finished our meals, walked back to the headquarters, and started saying our goodbyes. He thanked me again for my kind letter, and I thanked him for his time and generosity. He shook my hand and said, "Kev, it was an absolute pleasure. The food was great and the conversation was even greater." I smirked and cleverly responded, "Great? I'd say it was quite 'Majestic' and 'Divine." We both laughed and in that moment, I didn't care about not meeting my favorite teacher in elementary school, or some business folks in high school, or even some renowned professors in college. Because in that moment, I was the luckiest person alive. I finally won!

The Science Behind
Being Thankful

Thankfully, there is so much to be thankful for! It's all around us, in beautiful colors, marvelous shapes, dazzling sights, amazing people, and staggering inventions. Despite the robust world we live in, it is all too often that we take these people and things for granted. What if there was something we could do each day that could make us feel more connected to other people, and appreciate more things more often? What if there was something we could do that could make people feel valued, loved, complimented, positively influenced, and inspired?

Wouldn't it be amazing if we could feel more thankful for being alive? Well, here's the good news. All it takes is a single piece of paper and a little bit of gratitude, and it comes in the form of thank-you letters and gratitude journals.

A *Thank-You Letter* is a message that is crafted to make someone feel valued, cherished, and celebrated. Whether it is hand-written, typed, sent by mail, or sent by email, the core component of this kind of letter is to express deep flattery for the influence or inspiration that someone else has had on us. In the previous story, the letter I wrote to Andy was fueled by the impact his company had on my life. Through the vulnerability and veracity of the letter, Andy felt appreciated and inspired to keep serving as a health influencer. The bottom line is that these types of letters make people feel good about themselves. Having received some thank-you letters from past students, I can admit first-hand they brought a smile to my face and a sense of joy that I had never felt before.

Another tool to help us appreciate more of life is a *Gratitude Journal*. It's simple, we just have to write down three to five things we are thankful for at the end of each day. It only takes a couple of minutes, yet the impact it can have is huge. I decided to try this idea out for myself to see what might happen, and the outcome was extraordinary. Each night, I would pull out my little journal and write down three bullet-points of things that I appreciated. I tried to write down whatever came to mind, instead of the things I felt that I should be grateful for. I remember one night, specifically, I wrote down that I was thankful for my pillow, for allowing me to sleep comfortably every night. I laughed as I wrote it down because I thought it was silly to be thankful for something so trivial, but it turns out that the smallest things each day can have the biggest impacts in life. Other items I wrote down included my taste buds for giving me the ability to experience flavor, the cool breeze on a hot morning, the ocean for its beauty, and toothpaste for keeping my mouth clean. For the next week, I felt great after writing down items before bed, but I hadn't felt more appreciative during the day. Then, something magical happened. After about two weeks, I was taking a walk by the beach in the middle of the day, when the thought immediately popped into my head, "I'm so thankful for this right now, I'm going to write about this later!" It was a transformational moment, where the manufactured appreciation I was developing at night permeated into authentic appreciation in the middle of the day. As the days went on and I continued this journal, I started to feel an abundance of gratitude for small things *while* they were happening, instead of before bed while journaling. As I continue to journal each night, I continue to experience a default setting of gratitude each and every day.

One thing I am thankful for (see what I'm doing here?) is the fact that so much research has been done on gratitude. Social scientists have found that writing a thank-you letter can boost your happiness, reduce your depression, and increase the strength of your relationships[1,2,3,4]. Complimentary to professional help, therapy, and meditation, studies have actually shown that writing gratitude journals can help reduce anxiety[5]. Scientists at the University of Southern California discovered that gratitude stimulates parts of the brain that are linked with reward, empathy, and positivity[6]. Engaging in a daily practice of gratitude has even been found to increase alertness, enthusiasm, determination, attentiveness, energy, and sleep quality[7].

In a 10-week study, participants were required to either keep a gratitude journal (write down a few positive things), an irritation journal (write down a few negative things), or a neutral journal (write down whatever comes to mind). The results were fascinating. The people who wrote in the gratitude journal each night were happier, more optimistic, exercised more, and even visited the doctor less frequently[8]. By taking some time to be grateful, whether through a thank-you letter or gratitude journal, the body releases a feel-good chemical called, *Dopamine*[5]. Not only does this chemical help us feel a zing of happiness, it also encourages us to do whatever we just did again in the future[5]. By writing about what we are thankful for each day, and by writing letters to thank people who have helped us in life, we can hot-wire our brain to be more appreciative more often. Now that's something to be thankful for!

Typically, people take seemingly unimportant things for granted. For example, if someone was golfing on a day with nice weather, they probably wouldn't pay much attention to the wind. But, the moment a gust comes and moves their ball off-course, they'd get very frustrated. In other words, when things are easy, people don't really notice. But the moment things get difficult, it takes their full attention. What if it was the other way around? What if when things are going well, we could notice it and appreciate it? Then, when things get a little rough, we could find the good in it and still be thankful. For example, if the wind blew our ball off-course, we could still be thankful of the fact that we are spending some time outdoors, getting to play a fun game, enjoying the luxury of having golf clubs that were designed specifically for this use, stepping on grass that is so vibrantly green, and most likely spending some time with people we like. There's always some good to be found in everything.

Think about electricity as another example. Every single day, we plug our phones and computers into the wall to charge, we flip lights on and off as we enter and exit rooms, we grab fresh food from our refrigerators and freezers, we switch the TV on to get lost in shows and films, and we ride up and down giant buildings in elevators and escalators. But when something drastic happens like The Great Blackout of 2011, where seven million people in Southern California, Northern Parts of Mexico, and Western parts of Arizona all lost power, things start to change[9]. Everyday luxuries become survival necessities. When the power comes back on, everyone finds new joy in all the things they took for granted like lights, TV's, computers, elevators, and so on. Wouldn't it be great if there was a way to get that same sense of fresh enjoyment without having to experience the difficulty, destruction, or disaster? Well, according to scientific research and my personal experience, thank-you letters and gratitude journals are the perfect solution.

Thank-you letters even have the power to save someone's life. Paul, one of my students, came up to me after class one day and started crying. His grandpa had called him that morning to tell him that he was prepared to end his own life, but then he got Paul's thank-you letter and felt a profound new sense of purpose. He decided to keep living and keep pushing because of Paul's gratitude. Not only did Paul's grandfather feel valued and loved, Paul also felt the most connection he's ever felt with his grandpa. Not to mention, I started crying as Paul told me the story, which made me feel connected to both him and his grandfather. The power of a thank-you letter should never be underestimated.

With all of these benefits, it's a wonder as to why we aren't already writing thank-you letters and notes of gratitude every single day. One reason is that a lot of people aren't aware of all the positive potential. Another might be that people tend to shy away from sharing emotions and being vulnerable with friends, family, and even strangers. Expressing ourselves with transparency and honesty can be discomforting, which is why this exercise fits perfectly with our theme of becoming more comfortable with being uncomfortable. Regardless of what's holding us back, I think it's about time to see just how amazing it is to be grateful. And to think, it only takes a single piece of paper to get started.

Comfort Challenge 7: Be Thankful

We all have someone in our life who means a lot to us or has helped us greatly. It's about time we let them know how grateful we are! For this comfort challenge, you are invited to write a thank-you letter to someone who you are truly thankful for. The instructions are simple: write a letter, place it in an envelope with a stamp, and send it off!

Additional Challenge: Write three to five things you are thankful for before bed tonight. Don't feel the need to write things that you were *supposed* to be thankful for, just write whatever comes to mind. It could be as simple as seeing a butterfly cross your path or having enough gas to get where you were going. Then try it again the next night. Then again. It might only take a couple minutes each night, but the benefits are extraordinary!

8

The Dudes of Hazard

I suddenly woke up to the sound of a blaring horn outside my window. I nearly jumped out of bed as I opened my eyes and felt my heart pumping with shock. My bedroom looked blurry as I rubbed my tired eyes, and the horn went off again. It was a shrill, piercing sound that woke me up in a way that coffee never could. At first, I thought it was a mistake, but after several honks, I knew exactly who it was. I slid my window open and saw Torrin, my best friend, driving in circles around the cul-de-sac in his old, beat-up, white Ford Ranger. His head was out of the window like a dog in the summer, laughing hysterically, and he was slamming his steering wheel, honking the horn continuously. He yelled, "Rise and shine amigo! I know what we should do today." I grabbed a shirt, threw some pants on, and ran outside. Then, I screamed back, "Dude! You're going to wake the entire neighborhood, cut it out." He paused for a second, considered being courteous, then laughed and pressed his horn again, holding it until I was completely in his truck with my seatbelt on, ready to go. He flashed me a look that said, "That's what you get for telling me what to do." I tried to send him a look back that said, "You're nuts," but I'm not sure if it was sent exactly as I intended. Then we sped down my driveway, took a couple turns, and headed onto the highway.

The truck bumped and trotted down the road. "Where are we going anyway?" I asked. He creepily turned toward me and replied with a devilish grin, "I thought you'd never ask. I was bored this morning and was trying to decide what to do when I had a great idea." I interrupted, "Wait, how were you bored this morning, it's only 7am?" He put his finger up in the air and said, "Kev, come on. Okay? …Anyway, I was thinking about going to the skate park in Ocean Beach or going surfing in La Jolla, but I was watching this movie and had a better idea. The guy was riding this badass motorcycle through explosions and shooting bunnies on the side of the road, and I thought to myself, 'Why don't I have one of those?' So, we're going to go get me a motorcycle." A million questions ran through my mind. Why was he up so early? What movie was he watching that had a guy shooting bunnies? Where did he get the money for a new motorcycle? Where were we going right now to get one? Why was he so crazy? Instead, I decided to ask the only question that mattered: "Why didn't we think of this sooner?"

It turns out that he had found a rad motorcycle on Craigslist, a 1984 Honda Ascot to be exact, and the seller gave him the address of Gillespie Field, which was a tiny airport in Eastern San Diego. I jokingly asked, "When you said that you wanted to get a motorcycle, did you accidentally mean that you wanted to get a plane?" He laughed, parked the truck, took the keys out, and said, "Don't be ridiculous. Now come on, let's go." We reached the gate, punched in some numbers on a keypad, and waited for a response.

Through the garbled, crackling speaker of the security system, a manly voice came on and said, "I'll be right out."

Spruced up in a tilted golf cap, a button-down shirt, and a pair of Wrangler jeans, the craigslist seller we were meeting smelled of musky cologne and shaving cream. We walked a few hundred feet, around some parked bi-planes, and arrived at his "home away from home." It was an old, rusty airplane hangar that he had converted into a working garage. He assured us that it was more of an underground clubhouse like the ones for high rollers in Las Vegas. Then, he opened the aluminum garage door, and we realized he wasn't kidding. Eight beautiful motorcycles, one huge bi-plane, a few couches, a couple small TV's, and one very creepy lady mannequin all had their rightful place within his clubhouse.

As Torrin and Gary, the motorcycle-selling gentleman, started to talk about the bike for sale, I took advantage of my time alone to wander around the garage. Sure enough, I found some interesting things. Old archived newspaper clippings about politics, letters from past lovers and friends, and various historic photos of Gary when he was our age. After a few minutes, I was a little concerned about getting caught for rummaging, so I quickly headed out of the garage to where they were poking around the bike. It sure was beautiful. A very well-kept, jet-black Honda Ascot with a procured engine, redesigned foot pegs, and a new gas tank cover. All for just $1,500 measly dollars. Before having a chance to say yes or no, Gary interjected, "Alright you two, I'm going to give you a challenge. I'll bet you can't find a bike like this for the price anywhere else. If you're up for it, I'll hold onto the bike for two weeks and you can go have yourselves a look at what's on the market. But I assure you, you will be back." Torrin, quick to not be suppressed by the seniority of this man, replied, "Well, hold on. I don't care about other bikes on the market, but I do want to test drive it before I hand over the cash." And with that, Torrin borrowed a helmet, hopped into the saddle, and rode off on a motor with the power of 47 horses combined.

Meanwhile, Gary and I were forced to make small talk. He mentioned he had a date with a woman at a nearby coffee shop in just an hour or so. He then let me in on a little secret. "Let me tell you something kid. What you need to know is that women from the

Philippines are the best women out there. They'll love you the way a man should rightfully be loved, they'll worship the ground you walk on. Take it from me, I've dated a lot of women - because let's be honest, what woman doesn't love a man who can put a throbbing, vibrating engine between her legs?" My jaw dropped and I tried to avoid eye contact, but he curled his head around right back in front of mine. Then, he continued with a flare in his eye, "And out of all the beautiful Bettie's I've been with, I've never felt the loving squeeze quite like a Filipino woman." He creepily stared at me as he finished his raunchy rant. I took a step backward, to avoid both his closeness and his breath, and kindly told him, "Gary, thanks for sharing but I actually already have a girlfriend." His face lit up with excitement, "Oh! Great! Is she Filipino? I bet she's a fine piece of Filipino fun, nice going kiddo." Then he tried to rub my hair like I was his young grandson. I'm still not sure why I didn't just end the conversation right then and there. But, I was foolish and responded, "No, she's actually Polish and German." "What!" His face scrunched up. He was clearly taken aback. With a stern expression, he said, "Well then, she is no good. You'll have to throw her out and get another. I'm telling you kid, I'm not wrong on this. Those Polish and Germans... well you've heard of World War II haven't ya?" Thankfully, as if it was perfectly timed, Torrin came speeding back with his mouth open, tongue flapping, and a smile like a small child at a toy store. He killed the motor and shouted, "I'll take it!"

Thus began the arduous journey of getting both Torrin's old, bangy Ranger truck and his new, whippy motorcycle back to his house about 20 miles away. We decided that I would drive his truck while he would take his motorcycle. Thinking of his safety, I asked him, "How about you follow close behind me so that way if anything goes wrong, I'm right there. Sound good?" Torrin, obviously in a hurry, barely replied, "Yeah, let's go already!"

So, here's the thing. Torrin had a ton of experience with dirt bikes and BMX bikes, but this was about to be his first time ever riding a full-sized motorcycle on busy streets and the highway. Naturally, I was a little nervous about everything. "What about a helmet? And pads? Aren't you supposed to wear pants and long sleeves? Are you sure you should do this?" I asked. Frustrated, he looked up to the sky and let out a huge sigh. "Dude, I have my full-face BMX helmet (not DOT certified), I'll be fine without pads and sleeves (not smart), and of course I'm ready, I grew up riding a motorcycle (not a real motorcycle)." He hopped up on his bike with just his swim trunks and a short-sleeve T-shirt, a BMX helmet, snowboard goggles, and a grin from ear to ear. He revved the engine, and yelled, "Let's go!" This was clearly not Torrin's first comfort challenge.

As we raced down the freeway, I checked my rear-view mirror. There he was, right behind me, shaking and wobbling with his t-shirt whipping in the wind and his board-shorts inflating like balloons. I noticed several cars slowing down as they passed him to get a better look. One driver actually pulled out his cell phone to take photos and videos. Then, I watched as Torrin lifted an arm in the air and waved it up and down. He looked like a hero in a movie claiming victory, except he also looked like a surfer who had taken one too many waves to the head. Then, he started to get speed wobbles. At first, I thought it was just the road causing him to wiggle back and forth. After several seconds, I realized it wasn't the road at all. He shook violently back and forth. I didn't know what to do. I clicked my blinker to change to the slower lane, but there was a car in the way. I let my foot off the gas and hoped it would encourage him to do the same. Then, like a mad man, he sped up and split the lane right between me and the other car, shaking the entire way. As he passed me, he whipped his head to the side, and I could see him laughing under his facemask. He yanked the throttle and went even faster as he pulled in front of me and sped off. I chuckled with disbelief and thought to myself, "What a lunatic!"

After we pulled off the freeway and up to his house, I hopped out of the truck excited to hear all about his ride. He ripped his helmet off and shouted, "That was the craziest thing I've ever done! Woo! Oh my freaking god dude, I've never had so much adrenaline in my whole life! C'mon, you gotta try it!" Immediately, the words of my mom and dad started to echo in my mind. "You will never ride one of those death traps," my mom told me while I was growing up. "You know Kev, everyone I know who's ridden a motorcycle has ended up crashing and getting hurt," my dad told me when I was young. I wasn't even on it yet and I could feel adrenaline ripping through my whole body. I was nervous as hell and wanted to back down. Which is exactly why I decided to go for it.

I grabbed his BMX helmet, his snowboarding goggles, and threw on a long-sleeve T-shirt... safety first, right? I saddled up, kicked the motor on, and started goosing the throttle. At least, that's how I wish it happened. Instead, I slowly lifted my leg over the side of it, tilted back and forth, and almost fell over. I had no idea what I was doing. I had ridden a quad (ATV) and a tiny dirt bike once before, but nothing like this. The whole engine was shaking violently and vibrating beneath me. Torrin shouted from the side, "Okay, so that's the clutch. You have to kick up to shift up and kick down to shift down. Take it easy when you start, alright dude?"

I pulled the throttle back, kicked it into gear, revved the engine, yelled as I was ready to blast off... and stalled it. Torrin scowled at me, "Dude! You're going to mess it up. I'll give you another try but I don't want the gearbox to get wrecked." Afraid of letting my best friend down, I dropped my focus to a narrow vision. It was as if everything around me became blurred. It was just me and the motorcycle. I lightly tugged the throttle and kicked it into gear. Almost immediately, my head was thrown back and I blasted off down the road in what felt like a rocket ship. Immediately, I swerved like crazy and could barely hold on. I took a curving right turn, another sharp right turn, then I was blessed with a straightaway.

Hauling ass, kicking gears as if I'd known how to do it my whole life, I reached third gear and about 70 miles per hour in a 35mph speed limit area. My hair was absolutely frantic, my eyes were watery beneath the goggles, and every muscle in my body was shaking from fear, excitement, and the rumbles of the engine. Houses were blurry as they passed on either side of me, and I worried for any pedestrians that might be nearby. I bounced over potholes and speed bumps, which felt like stuntman ramps. All the advice my parents gave me started to echo in my mind. What was I doing? Was I crazy? Then it hit me. I didn't know how to slow down! I had never down-shifted or stopped before. Was it pull the clutch and then pedal up? Or pedal down? Panic set in. My arms started to wobble as I tried to come up with a plan. Barely avoiding parked cars and nearly hitting the sidewalk, I decided to yank the brake and hope for the best. The tires locked and the bike skidded across the street. I held on for dear life. After wobbling and swerving about, I finally came to a complete stop. It was a miracle. The bike was okay. I was okay. The motorcycle was still, but my heart raced liked an Olympic sprinter. My breaths were rapid and labored. I looked around at the neighborhood and noticed I was already on the other side of town. I rested my head down on the handlebars and took a moment to be thankful for making it out alive. This was one of the scariest moments of my life, yet I felt an incredible sense of freedom and gratitude. Sure, it was an unusual place to be, but I found comfort in the shock. I fired the engine back up, gently pulled the throttle, and scooted slowly in the direction I came from, with a giant smile on my face.

I took a few more turns to circle back around, and landed back at Torrin's house. Considering my miraculous survival, I felt as if I could do anything at this point. Then, I suddenly made a huge and careless mistake. Feeling like I knew exactly what I was doing, I attempted a smooth parking job right next to the sidewalk. While slowing down, I nudged it down to neutral, braked improperly, and the whole bike toppled over to the side. Torrin screamed from his driveway. With all of my might, I planted my feet and held onto the handlebars, trying desperately to keep it from crashing over. I managed to slow it down, but it still crashed onto the side of the handlebar enough to bend it. With my entire body acting as a single muscle, I pulled the bike back up. Torrin inspected the damage and said, "You are so lucky man, I thought for sure it was going to get wrecked." I let out a huge sigh of relief, "I'm so sorry man! I'll pay to get it fixed." He looked at it again, let out a small laugh, and replied, "Don't worry about it, it'll give me something to do next time I'm bored."

The Science Behind Adrenaline-Rushes

What do job interviews, public presentations, salary negotiations, first dates, marriage proposals, skydiving, and driving a motorcycle for the first time all have in common? Adrenaline! No matter where we go in life, at some point we'll be faced with a situation that spikes our adrenaline levels. Adrenaline, also known as *Epinephrine*, is a hormone that is sparked by strong emotions and "synchronizes the mind and body to take on the stresses of the outside world"[1]. Most people know this hormone as the "fight or flight" experience, which means adrenaline prepares us for battle or for escape, depending on the situation. Whether it might be meeting new people, a social gathering, or kayaking over a waterfall, it is not necessarily a bad thing to experience these types of emotional responses. On the contrary, we can use these chemical spikes to our advantage. Challenging ourselves beyond what is comfortable is a way to develop greater skills, and increases the likelihood that we will experience more presence in our lives[2]. Adrenaline can even be thought of as a shortcut to mindfulness, because it fine-tunes our senses, heightens our awareness of everything that is happening around us, and minimizes the barrage of useless thoughts that we are used to.

Back in the 1970s, a researcher conducted a global survey asking people when they felt and performed their best, and more specifically, "What makes a life worth living?" Throughout the study, his team interviewed over 8,000 people, including CEOs, Olympic athletes, business founders, Himalayan climbers, Navajo shepherds, blind nuns, poets, musicians, and artists. The overarching discovery was that people felt the most pleasure, and performed at their highest levels, when experiencing a seamless connection between the body, mind, and environment[2]. This kind of synchronicity is often a result of adrenaline releases and chemical spikes in our bodies, also known as *Physiological Arousal*[3]. States of arousal can occur whether we are nervous or excited -- jumping from a plane, asking for a raise, giving a speech, proposing to our lover, or pitching an invention. The trick to lessening fear and fueling excitement is to recognize that our bodies have the same reaction, regardless of whether our mind thinks it's positive or negative, and to adopt a mindset that favors opportunities over obstacles.

Once we recognize this and take steps to frame our fears as possibilities, we can push ourselves to higher levels than we ever thought possible. Scientists call this practice *Anxiety Reappraisal*, which can be as simple as reframing the self-talk that happens just before a big event[4]. Instead of thinking, "I'm so nervous for this speech," we can tell ourselves, "I'm so excited for this chance to share my message." Instead of saying to ourselves, "I'm scared I might not get the job at the interview today," we can say, "I'm going to gain some great experience in this interview today, regardless of what happens." We'll still feel the butterflies, jitters, and sweats, but we're building a new relationship with ourselves that highlights courage, curiosity, and acceptance. In this way, our mind and body can seamlessly work together to help us succeed.

Want to know a secret? Extreme athletes, such as skydivers, base-jumpers, speed-boaters, dirt-bikers, and skateboarders, aren't actually fearless[5]. Similarly, many public speaking professionals come from a background of stage fright[6]. On top of that, many highly energetic performers prefer to spend most of their time quietly resting[7]. How do people who are scared of heights jump from planes, and people who are scared of the stage give standing ovation speeches? The answer is simple. They were able to use fear, instead of being abused by it. They got more familiar with the physical responses that take place during high levels of stress, such as sweaty palms, heavy breathing, and butterflies, and adapted their mindset to shift from impossibility to possibility[5,8]. They got more familiar with what it felt like to be scared, both mentally and physically, and adapted to their own adrenaline. Instead of saying to themselves, "I can't," they continuously repeated, "I CAN!"

Take Alex Honnold for example, a man who has defied gravity by climbing huge cliffs without any ropes. Honnold is often referred to as "history's greatest ever climber in the free solo style"[9]. He scaled the giant rock-wall known as Half-Dome in Yosemite and even walked along a sliver of rock 1,800 feet high (aptly referred to as the "Thank-God Ledge") without ropes or safety gear. Recently, his brain was studied by scientists via an MRI machine, and they found that his response to dangerous situations was less than other young men his age. Yet, Honnold admits to being afraid and getting scared. Instead of chalking it up to genes or disorders, scientists believe it has more to do with his repeated exposure over time[9]. Even though he feels afraid, he has become familiar with the feeling and has learned how to use that energy in a positive way. By doing something that makes us a little uncomfortable several times with the right attitude, we have the opportunity to become more comfortable with it[10]. While this is a common technique in overcoming fear, and is often referred to as *Exposure Therapy*, our purpose is to focus on exposing ourselves to conditions that are fun and safe, not overwhelming or dangerous. It is important to point out that exposure therapy only works when small steps are taken over a longer period of time, and if you experience extreme phobias or serious anxiety issues, professional help may be the best course of action.

Not only was Honnold's repetition of discomfort important in his success, but it also took trying new climbs that were more difficult each time. Each climb made him a little more uncomfortable than the previous one, but each time he succeeded, he expanded his realm of possibility. This is similar to our exploration in toddlerhood, where we roll until we can crawl, stumble until we can walk, and trot until we can run. In fact, Dr. Dan Siegel, a best-selling author and world-renowned neurobiologist, describes this idea of experimentation as one of the four essential components of life[11]. Trying new things, exposing ourselves to new situations, having curiosity, and raising the bar each time can be incredibly rewarding and is at the core of what makes our lives feel fulfilling[10].

It is not just about taking risks, it's about taking *Calculated Risks*. People who take too big of a risk too quickly often become risk-avoidant, which means they are less likely to experiment in the future[12]. However, people who appraise their situation with rational thinking and a methodical approach, instead of emotional reaction and a reckless approach, increase their likelihood of success and increase future beneficial risks[13]. An article in The New York Times suggests that seeking new adventures helped our species survive and grow[14]. Think about it. Why did ancient sailors travel across the world to unknown destinations? Why did ancient explorers forge their way into new forests, hike over untouched mountaintops, and wade through uncharted rivers? The reason is that doing things we've never done before is how we learn, grow, and foster the future ahead of us.

The best part is that repeated exposure to adrenaline, or stressful situations, is a process that transcends from one aspect of life to another. Even though we might climb rocks, meet strangers, or sing songs in public as a form of exposure, it has the potential to teach us how to respond to any stressful situation in the future. This is a strategy often employed by the military, where they use scenarios and mock situations to prepare soldiers for what they might experience during an actual battle[15]. According to David Swink, a threat management expert, "Many people discover that the more they are able to successfully accomplish adrenaline-spiking activities, the easier it is to think clearly, react effectively, listen, and breathe during other intense experiences"[15]. By engaging in a thrill or adventure several times with baby steps, it has the potential to make other seemingly scary things easier, like public speaking, job interviews, salary negotiations, and relationship conflicts. Which, is really the essence of this entire book: to step out of the familiar and explore the unfamiliar, to break away from what we know to find out what we don't, and to become more comfortable with being uncomfortable. So, whether it's bungee-jumping from a bridge, dancing with a stranger, pitching a new business idea, moving to a new place, or any other situation that spikes adrenaline levels, it's not nerve-wracking, it's exciting!

Comfort Challenge 8: Adrenaline-Rush

It's time to get your heart pumping! For this challenge, do something that you know will excite you. Maybe it's skydiving, flying in a helicopter, swimming with dolphins, going on a rollercoaster, asking a stranger for their phone number, or even riding a motorcycle. Regardless of what you do, make sure it is safe. For example, if you are going to cliff-jump into water, double-check the water depth and that it is clear of rocks. If you are delivering an expensive sales pitch to wealthy investors, double-check that your proposal is free of embarrassing typos. If you're going to flirt with someone new, double-check that your zipper is up. Ultimately, if you are going to take a risk, make it a *Calculated Risk*. Oh, and don't forget to enjoy the ride!

9

Nervous Number-Twos

I stood on stage, completely alone, in front of a huge crowd of people watching me. The room was packed and silent while they waited for me to start. Nervous as hell, my hands were shaking and my heart was racing. I was about to play a song for everyone that I hadn't even written yet. I had no formal training on piano, and I was about to perform for the first time. They waited like vultures, hungry for entertainment. I could feel my stomach turn upside-down. This might have been the most nerve-wracking moment of my entire life. I closed my eyes, took a deep breath, and felt like I was going to puke.

Earlier that day, I walked into a cozy little coffee shop during my lunch break in San Jose. The place was artfully decorated with local canvas paintings on the walls. Warm, yellow lights hung from the ceiling and gave the room an incandescent glow. The entire room smelled like fresh roasted coffee beans and delicious pastries. There was a second story loft where people were enjoying their warm drinks and playing games. In the corner of the shop, there was a dusty, old piano that looked like it hadn't been played in years. I waved for the barista's attention, "Hey, would it be okay if I played that piano?" She nodded, "Of course! We'd love it if you did." I stepped over to it and lifted the key cover. Dust erupted from beneath the cloth, and the white keys were covered in a sheet of gray. I hadn't played in a few months so I figured I was probably as rusty as the piano's insides. Pressing down on one of the keys, I heard a beautiful sound that contradicted how the piano looked. It was like finding a magical, forgotten book in a rickety, old attic, opening up to the first page, and entering a wonderful new world of imagination. I pressed more keys and fell further into the new world. More keys, and I started to get really into it. Even more keys, and I was completely lost in a musical land with no map and a heart set on exploration. At least, that's how it was in my mind. If you had actually seen me at the coffee shop that day, you would have seen me with my eyes closed, hunched over the piano, slamming down on the keys like I was trying to break them, and rocking my head wildly around like an angry teenager listening to oversized headphones.

In the midst of this musical escapism, I felt someone tap me on the shoulder and I near jumped out of the seat. Letting off the keys, I turned around. "Excuse me," an old gentleman said. He had gray hair that resembled the dust on the keys. The hair was on top of his head, coming out of his ears, hanging down from his nose, and sticking out from all sides of his face. "You are quite good, my boy." He smiled and told me his name was Charlie, then continued, "Say, son, how would you like to headline for our live music night tonight? You see, I own this place and I gotta tell you, you've got real talent. We'd love to have you play for everyone. Whaddya say?" Still trying to bridge the real world in front of me and the lost world I was just in, I just sat there for a moment. He continued to nod along, waiting for an answer. Finally, even though I was excited and nervous as hell, I shook his hand and said, "Sounds great."

Here's the thing, I grew up playing music most of my life. When I was eleven years old, some friends asked if I wanted to be in a band. I didn't play any instruments at the time, so I told them that I wouldn't be of much use. The bassist told me on a Friday that it was fine, and to just learn how to play guitar by Monday. To clarify, what he told me was to learn how to competently play a musical instrument that some people spend their entire life studying and mastering, in just three days. At the time, though, I was a kid with big eyes and even bigger vision. I immediately went home to my dad that night and asked if he could teach me how to play guitar over the next few days. Instead of telling me I was crazy, stupid, or that it was impossible, he smiled and said in his wacky, Boston accent, "Okay, let's get started, Kev."

As it turns out, playing guitar is really difficult. It takes way more than a few days to learn. After putting in almost eight hours each of those days, the only difference between the Monday and the previous

Friday, was that I could play the first three notes of *Smoke on the Water*. Needless to say, my friends hadn't gotten much better at their instruments either.

Skipping ahead, I had taken lessons for nearly two years, practiced nearly every day, and continued to hone my craft. I became the lead guitarist for several bands. By a stroke of luck, I even got hired as a professional musician in Los Angeles for about a year (between you and me, it was for a pop singer that used to be part of a very popular boy band. Our biggest fans were 12-year-old girls, so I'm equally proud and embarrassed of this achievement). By the time I was 25, I had gone on mini-tours and played live shows all over the country, including venues like the House of Blues, The Whiskey a Go-Go, The El Rey Theater, The Roxy, and even the world-famous San Diego Zoo.

At first, performing was terrifying. When I was 15 and in my first band, I hid behind the giant P.A. speakers on stage and played most of my parts wrong. It was awful. But after more and more shows, I became more and more comfortable with being uncomfortable. At one point, I stepped up on the ledge of the stage and stepped out onto the head of someone in the crowd. The fan grabbed my foot and held it on his head while

I played the solo intro to the song. I truly felt like a rock-star.

But there's safety in numbers. The comfort I had developed while playing concerts always came from the fact that my closest friends were on stage with me. Anytime I felt overwhelmed or scared, I could turn to one of them and it would all be okay. But, I had never played music in front of people alone.

So, sitting there in that coffee shop and being asked to play piano, which isn't even my main instrument, alone as the headliner for a live music night, was absolutely terrifying. As far as playing piano, I was self-taught and didn't think I was very good. I didn't know scales, notes, octaves, signatures, how to read music, the theory of music, or anything. I just liked the feeling of pushing keys and hearing notes that sounded good. I literally didn't even know how to play a whole song. Agreeing to play live piano that night was a whole new level of terrifying.

My lunch break at the coffee shop was ending, and I needed to get back to the jobsite for the rest of my shift. I thanked the baristas for the food, said goodbye to Charlie, and told him I'd see him that night. I walked back to the conference center where I was working, and pretty much shook the entire way with nervousness. I kept getting chills thinking about the idea of being up in front of a room full of people, all alone. I didn't know if I could actually do it.

Work felt like it took forever. Trying to type was a challenge as my fingers vibrated with electricity (having been electrocuted before, I know the feeling quite well, but that's another story for another time). Feeling pretty bashful, I kept excusing myself to the restroom because nervousness had a way of shaking me up and cleaning me out (with what I aptly refer to as the *'Nervous Number-Twos'*). Finally, it was time to clock out. I headed to my hotel room, showered, changed, and made my way out to the coffee shop. While I was strolling over, I was listening to headphones to calm down. I convinced myself there was no way it'd be crowded because it was a weeknight, and the coffee shop was pretty small. I figured there might be one or two people besides the baristas and Charlie.

Boy, was I wrong. As I walked through the door of Caffe Frascati's, I saw a much bigger crowd than I anticipated. They must have been breaking every fire code in the building because people were lined along the walls, crowded on the upstairs terrace, sat in rows of chairs in front of the stage, up on tables to make more space, and even seated outside on the patio facing inward. It was like a mini version of Madison Square Garden on a sold-out night. I nervously walked past several of the people, bumping many along the way. I approached the barista and ordered a minty tea, hoping the ancient yogis were right that mint leaves had relaxing properties. After a couple minutes, I grabbed my tea and took a seat.

The host of the evening, who had long dreaded hair, flowy hemp pants, an oversized t-shirt, and looked as though he had taken one too many drugs in his lifetime, took the stage and said with a slur, "Hello, hello, everyone! My name is Buddy, welcome to the, uhh, show!" He started laughing at himself while rocking back and forth. He continued, "We've got some amazing, uhh, performers tonight and wait, wait, wait, do you guys feel that?" I looked around at everyone wondering if there was an inside-joke that I wasn't getting, and everyone else seemed just as confused as I was. I looked back toward the host and he laughed, "The vibes man! Whoa, there's some good vibes here tonight. Let's get started with the first performer, her name is, uhh, Jacklyn, and she is going to read us her poem. Oh my gosh, I love poems! Jacklyn, come on up."

Jacklyn took the stage and did exactly that, she read us her poem. Word for word. Without looking up once from her piece of paper, she stood at the mic and read aloud without moving. She went over the five minute limit and approached the 10-minute mark. I looked to the host, who usually has the task of keeping performers within their allotted time. He was sitting with his eyes closed, sort of bobbing his head up and down. I wasn't sure if he fell asleep or was really enjoying the poem. Either way, this was good news for me. If all the performers were at this level, then my rookie piano skills would make me seem like Elton John or Billy Joel!

Finally, after about 12 minutes, Jacklyn stopped speaking and ran back to her seat. There were some claps and some murmurs. While some people chuckled and whispered, I couldn't help but feel really proud of her for having the bravery to go up in front of everyone alone. I gave her a high-five as she walked past me and told her she did a great job.

Buddy took the stage again and clapped, "Whoa, whoa, whoa. Beautiful vibes, Jacky, beautiful vibes. Let's give it up for our next set of performers, Justin and Jake." Two guys with guitars approached the stage and sat side-by-side. Secretly hoping for them to be even worse than Jacklyn, I watched as they tuned their guitars. A few moments later, one of them started strumming and the other started playing a lead riff on top. It sounded incredible. They did a cover of *Just The Way You Are*, by Bruno Mars, and their performance was amazing, just like the lyrics in the song. In a matter of minutes, the entire audience was singing and clapping along. Sweat was pouring down their faces as they sang and played with such emotion. Sweat was pouring down my face as well, but for an entirely different reason. As they finished, the crowd cheered and clapped and even gave a standing ovation. "Well, so much for them crashing and burning," I thought to myself. I was in real trouble now.

Several other performers took the stage, some absolutely amazing and some just okay. After about an hour, Buddy took the front of the stage and announced that it was time for the last performer, me. "Everyone, everyone, you still with me? Let's keep the energy flowing and the grooves going, for our headliner tonight we have, uhh, Kevin, who is going to be playing piano for us. Good vibes man, good vibes!" The room erupted in applause while I made my way to the stage.

Sitting at the piano, my heart was racing. Just like before, my fingers were buzzing and now more than ever, I could feel a 'Nervous Number Two' coming on. Buddy asked me if I needed anything and I jokingly told him that I would just need an ambulance if I passed out. He laughed hysterically, more than anyone has laughed at anything I've ever said, and walked to the back of the room. There I was. All alone, up in front of a huge crowd of people, sitting at an instrument that I really didn't know how to play all that well. On my list of moments that scared the living shit out of me, literally, this was at the top. I immediately felt like Billy Joel as the Piano Man. The crowd was in the mood for a melody and it was my job to make them feel alright. I tried to buy some time by pretending to stretch my fingers. Still not ready, I reached up and stretched my body. Everyone was watching. Everyone was waiting.

I pressed down the first key and the piano sang out beautifully. Just one key at a time, I told myself.

Pushing down the second key, a melody started to form. I closed my eyes and let everything go. Instead of worrying about people watching me, instead of worrying about messing up, I just listened to the gorgeous sound of the strings inside the piano. Getting lost in the sounds, I kept my eyes closed and started to nod my head along; up and down to the ups and downs of the melody. Pressing harder and harder, I felt all of my emotions pouring out onto the keys, and I let it take over. No more nervousness, no more shaking, no more fright. Just pure joy.

As the song I was making up on the spot progressed to a slower part, I turned and looked toward the crowd. To my surprise, nearly everyone in the room had their eyes closed, and they were swaying their heads to the music. In that moment, I felt connected to everything. To the people watching, to the music, to the piano, to Buddy, to Justin and Jake, to the people on the patio, to Billy Joel, and to the entire universe. Minutes passed and I slowed down on the keys, delicately pressing them as I ended the song. For a few seconds, the room sat in complete silence. The only sounds came from the espresso machines and coffeemakers whirring and buzzing. Then, in an explosion, the entire room burst with claps and cheers.

I learned a huge lesson that night. Being exposed to uncomfortable situations, completely alone, was by far one of the most rewarding things I had ever done. I had found a great sense of comfort in yet another unusual place. Don't get me wrong, it is great to have friends along the way. But, entering an uncomfortable space alone is really where the magic starts to happen. Or should I say, it's really where the *music* starts to happen.

The Science Behind Flying Solo

L et's imagine we're in an airplane, flying across the sky at 700 miles an hour, and suddenly one of the engines goes out. Turbulence starts to kick up in the cabin and people begin to panic. The oxygen masks suddenly drop from the ceiling and the flight attendants are worriedly directing everyone to put them on. We have just a few seconds to make a decision that will save our lives. Next to us, there is a small child who clearly can't reach the mask. Who do we put the mask on first, ourselves or the small child?

If you answered yourself, you are not selfish, and you are definitely not a terrible person. In fact, you made the right choice, according to every airline safety demonstration ever given. While the science behind airplane safety is not within the scope of this book, it serves as a fascinating example for the old adage, "you have to help yourself before you can help others." This same idea is found in several other areas, such as mountain-rescue teams, lifeguarding, scuba diving, and sports teams.

Gaining independence is not just helpful in the midst of crisis and catastrophe, it is also good for our brain and body. In fact, it is so good for us that the United States declared a Wilderness Act back in 1964 that required "outstanding opportunities for solitude" in natural land[1]. It is a federal law that we have space to spend time alone in nature. An article released from the University of Massachusetts suggests that the benefits of solitude, including freedom, creativity, and spirituality, outweigh the detriments[2]. In order to find true harmony and balance in our social life, we need to experience disengaged time from other people[3]. Scientists refer to this as the *Connection-Autonomy Dialectical Tension*, which is the idea that we have a fundamental need for connecting with other people and spending time alone[4]. Our ability to succeed in social settings stems from the confidence, esteem, and resilience of self-reflection. So, in order to experience greater connection, we need to first experience greater independence.

As one researcher puts it, becoming mentally healthy is synonymous with becoming more confidently independent[5]. It is important to highlight the idea that independence is not about being a loner or condemned to isolation, it is about having confidence in ourselves and our relationships[5]. Specifically, this entire chapter is built on the idea that solitude is time spent engaged with oneself and disengaged from the heavy influence of others. This is called *Relative Social Disengagement*, which means that we can still experience solitude even when other people are around us[2]. For example, if we are writing, reading, or reflecting in a coffee shop, there are other people within our public space, but we are still engaging in solitude. In the last story, while I was playing piano for the public, I was experiencing a state of self-engagement and social disengagement. I became lost in the music to the point that I felt completely alone. It wasn't until the music stopped and I opened my eyes that I remembered the crowd of people around me.

What is truly fascinating is that we are hard-wired for independence at a young age. We engage in self-guided exploration, sometimes before we even have the ability to poop in a toilet. One of the tenants of toddlerhood is the development of bodily abilities, such as walking, trotting, and stumbling around like a little drunk person, all of which start us on the journey toward self-discovery. Think about it, toddlers are always running off in every direction away from their mother. According to the University of Illinois, this is a natural part of gaining social and emotional growth[6]. As toddlers start to explore, they gain confidence in their independence and also start to realize how important their relationship with their mother truly is. In the same way, when we explore independently as adults we build our self-confidence and self-esteem, and recognize the importance of our relationships.

Some of the important benefits of solitude, as noted by researchers, are freedom and creativity[2]. Specifically, when we engage in activities alone we have two types of freedom: the freedom from constraints, and the freedom to engage in desired activities. We've all been in a situation where we wanted to do one thing, but other people we were with wanted to do something else. In most cases, because of a psychological influence effect called Groupthink or Herd Mentality, we end up just doing whatever the group wants to do[7,8]. In one such example, while I was at a music festival in Iceland, I really wanted to see an artist at the beautiful Harpa music hall. The other people I was with had more of an urge to see a punk band at a bar. Falling to the influence of the herd, I ended up following along to the bar. The band ended up being terrible, the whole place smelled like old beer and dried vomit, and we left halfway through the set. I was beyond bummed. Meanwhile, I found out later in a festival review that the performance I wanted to see at Harpa was rated as one of the top shows of the year. If I had explored independently during those few hours, I would have been able to see one of the most spectacular performances of the festival! Similarly, when I played piano by myself in the coffee shop, I didn't have to confine my musical style to the pressure of other musicians, which is something I was familiar with from playing in so many bands with other people.

Instead, I had complete creative freedom, which was intoxicatingly freeing. Doing some things alone helps us lift limitations from others and open opportunities for ourselves.

In regard to creativity, it turns out that daydreaming and self-reflecting are important tools in the development of new ideas. Here's how it works: When we disengage from external stimuli, such as being around other people, we become more sensitive to what's going on inside ourselves. We start to become more aware of shifting emotions, and more importantly, we become more exposed to new thoughts, new ideas, and alternative perspectives on reality[9]. Interestingly enough, a study from two different teams in Antarctica describes the importance of solitude in relation to creativity[10]. One team consisted of people who were kept isolated from each other in small tents, while the other team spent most of the time working together and collaborating in the same space. By the end of the three weeks, team solitude scored higher on a creativity scale than the other team. Specifically, the solitude team reported that their imagination could feel as strong as a good book or movie, and that even the slightest crackle of flames could stimulate daydreaming. To sum it up, spending some time away from other people once in a while can boost our imagination, inventiveness, and creativity.

The good news for team solitude is that it has acquired many popular and famous sponsors throughout history. First and foremost, spiritual guides and gurus including Jesus, Buddha, Moses, and Gandhi, all actively sought time alone in order to share their insight with the world. Famous writers including Ernest Hemingway, Henry David Thoreau, John Steinbeck, and Franz Kafka, have all referred to time in solitude as an inspiration for profound stories. Artists including Pablo Picasso and Leonardo da Vinci, musicians including Celine Dion and Eric Clapton, inventors including Thomas Edison and Steve Wozniak, and the musical magician behind *The Dark Knight* and *Interstellar* soundtracks, Han Zimmer, have all highlighted the importance of spending quality time alone as part of their success.

If you find yourself struggling when trying to spend some time by yourself, it turns out that you are not alone. In fact, a popular research study found that people were more likely to give themselves an electric shock than sit alone in stillness and silence[11]. In one such instance, a man shocked himself 190 times in less than a half hour because it was more stimulating than boredom[11]. It turns out that this is all for a good reason. According to a recently published book about the importance of belonging, if we didn't follow our tribe in the old days, we would most likely die[12]. But, things change. We don't live in tribal-based societies anymore, and we definitely wash our hair more often (well, at least some of us do). While too much alone time, specifically in the form of isolation or confinement, can be detrimental or destructive, a healthy dose of solitude is a great way to develop independence, freedom, creativity, and as a result, stronger connection with others. Doing things alone can naturally feel uncomfortable, which is why it nestles perfectly into this book. The goal of this chapter, and the comfort challenge that follows, is to help us identify a strategic way to try some things on our own as a tool for growth and development.

So, whether it is taking the stage as a public speaker, paddling to the line-up as a surfer, designing the next great billboard, teeing up as a golfer, or inventing the next big thing at home in your pajamas, it turns out that spending some time disconnected can actually make us feel more connected to ourselves, to others, and to everything around us. Just like the babies, toddlers, and children that crawl, trot, and navigate the new world around them, we can start to experience a new world around us when we curiously explore by ourselves. The good news for us is that we already know how to walk, we have access to cars and planes, and we are already (hopefully) potty-trained. It's time to see what the world has to offer!

Comfort Challenge 9: Fly Solo

For this comfort challenge, you are invited to do something alone that you would normally do with others*. If you'd like, you can think of it as taking yourself out on a fun date! As social creatures, we spend so much of our time plugged in to others, whether it is in-person, online, or over the phone. It's time to unplug and see just what it's like to discover, explore, and be curious along the way. If you're not sure what to do, here are some great examples:

- See a new movie at the theaters
- Try out a different restaurant
- Go to a quirky museum or unique store
- Take a walk in an area you've never been

*Note: If you're thinking to yourself that you already do all of these things alone, that's totally fine. Just flip the challenge and include other people!

10

The Cliffhanger

There I was, dangling upside-down 50 feet above the ground, suspended by a single rope. The sky was cracking and booming with thunder and lightning. The rock face in front of me was a jagged threat. My head pounded, my hands shook inside a pair of wet, leather gloves, and my body dangled helplessly. Panicked and trembling, I wrestled with the rope and different parts of the rock to try to flip myself back over. I was literally hanging on by a thread.

Earlier that week, I was hiking around some hills in the back country of Southern California, when I was approached by a team of burly men and women. They were dressed in red and black, and all of them had a big, red cross woven into their jackets. As they walked up, I noticed each of them had backpacks that were bigger than their bodies. The grizzly man in the front spoke up first, "Hey there, you like the outdoors?" I nodded, "Heck yeah. I'd live right here if I could." The stocky man smiled behind his scraggly beard, and the others around him smiled as well. The man stretched his arm out, shook my hand, and said, "We're recruiting for our mountain rescue team. You seem like a pretty good fit. How about you join us for a wilderness training this weekend to get a glimpse of what we do? You'll learn all kinds of cool outdoors lessons, like how to pack a sleeping bag really tight, how to build a shelter out of sticks, how to find a way out when you're lost, and even how to rappel off a cliff. What do you say?" My eyes widened and I nodded again. "That sounds amazing."

A few hours later, while at home, I laid out all of my wilderness belongings and tried to figure out exactly what I needed to pack. Even though I was an experienced hiker, climber, camper, and adventurer, I had never been audited by professionals. It's sort of like how we drive cars all the time and think we're great at it, but the moment we have a driving test (or our girlfriend's dad in the car), we start to overthink everything and screw up. The last thing I wanted was to be out there in the middle of the mountains and get laughed at for having the wrong gear. So, I continued to pack with keen eyes and a focused mind.

The trip was a two-day backpacking excursion and we were expected to bring enough food, water, clothes, and gear to take care of ourselves and at least one other person. Basically, we were to pack for two, but carry for one… Right. The majority of camping trips I had been on before, we had access to the car nearby, so it didn't really matter what we brought. At this point, I had only ever gone on one backpacking trip up in Big Sur, and I was rudely awakened by just how unprepared I was for three days with no resources. (To give a snapshot of that trip, I ran out of water and had to create a filter using my only pair of clean boxers tied over the spout of my water bottle… and I still got terribly sick!) Needless to say, I needed to be smarter about packing for the weekend trip ahead of me.

I started to rummage through the different items to figure out which were necessities, which were luxuries, and which were useless. Okay, umbrella? Useless. (Or so I thought...) Water filter? Necessity. Utility knife? Necessity. Machete? Probably not recommended. For food, I ended up packing two gallons of water, six protein bars, six granola bars, and some dried fruit for good measure.

For clothes, I didn't want to seem like a "glamper" or a "yuppee" (derogatory names for people who try to be glamorous while they camp), but the weather did call for cold temperatures and maybe a very light drizzle. So, I packed what I thought was just enough. Two pairs of boxers, two pairs of socks, two shirts, one jacket, one beanie, one pair of gloves, and one pair of boots. This would prove to be a mistake later.

For gear, I packed trekking poles (that still had the tag on them), a water filter with a compact, foldable canteen, a 2-person tent from Walmart (mistake), a tarp, a self-inflating sleeping pad, an old sleeping bag that I had in my garage, a utility knife that I bought at a swap meet, and a huge backpack that could probably fit a small child inside with room to spare. Things I wish I could have brought... a grill, a pillow, a rolling suitcase, and maybe a generator. But it was about time I got back to my roots again. It had been at least a few

months since my last camping trip, and as John Muir
would say (along with all the nature hipsters
nowadays), "The mountains were calling."

It was only a three hour drive to the destination out
in the Southern Californian mountains, just on the
other side of Palm Springs and tucked back near
Idyllwild. It was late evening, and the sun had slid
behind the faraway horizon. As I got out of the car, I
immediately looked around at everyone's gear to
compare what I brought. Some people had trekking
poles strapped to the side of their packs, others had
multiple carabiners and keychains dangling off the
front with various items like coffee mugs,
switchblades, rope, or gloves. It was crazy to think that
everything we needed for two to three days had to fit
in a single backpack.

I found the crew that I originally had met back on
the trail a few days ago and approached them. "Well
look who it is!" One of the taller ones called out as I
walked over. All of them, along with all of the others in
the lot, were dressed in bright orange, button-up shirts
that had an array of patches indicating their various
certifications. They all had headlights strapped to their
heads that were switched off for the moment. Ralph,

one of the shorter members of the crew, spoke up, "So, you decided to join us, that's great! I think you'll love getting to see what we do out here." "Yeah," I said as I nodded, "Thanks so much for the invite. I know this typically isn't something you offer... letting an outsider get an inside look at rescue training, so I'm really excited to see what's in store." The taller one, Jeremy, replied, "Just you wait, kid. It's like an obstacle course, cross-fit gym, and boot camp all-in-one for adventurers. Up for it?" I grinned, "Definitely." A nervous feeling started to brew in my stomach, but I was too damn curious to turn back now.

Not more than 20 minutes later, I was huffing and puffing as we continued to trek up the steepest trail I had ever hiked. The weather hung at a brisk 50 degrees, which made it a bit challenging to breathe. My backpack felt like it weighed at least 75 pounds, and I could feel indents in my shoulders where the straps continued to tug downward. This was an all-out mission to battle gravity. Not to mention my boots were brand new and the consequences of this decision were starting to hurt... I could feel the blisters forming already but we had about four more miles to go to our first rendezvous point! I did what all great hikers would do in this situation; I kept moving.

After what felt like half the night but was probably only a couple hours, we finally landed at the first meeting spot. I chucked my backpack off my shoulders and crumbled down to the ground. I'm pretty sure there wasn't a single spot on me that wasn't sweaty. Propping the pack up, I used it as a backrest and waited for the commander (the rescuer in charge of the operation) to give the next instructions. I looked to the others, and all I could see was the bright glow from their headlights, some red, some white, some yellow. Earl, the lead rescuer, stood in the center of our circle and made his announcements. We were to keep hiking for another two miles (seriously?!). Then we would be split into teams of four or five members, and each team would be given a set of specific GPS coordinates. As a team, we would walk another one to two miles to our specific camping site, set-up for the night, and get some sleep before our very early start the next morning. We did the only thing we could do at this point. We walked.

After a couple more hours, our coordinates took us to a random spot in the wilderness, off the trail by a few hundred feet. I looked around with just the small glow of my headlight. It seemed to be just dirt, leaves, trees, and sticks. I kicked around some rocks hoping to discover something miraculous. Apparently, I was foolish for thinking that a "camping site," as Earl had instructed us to find, would include some sort of signage, maybe an outhouse, or some kind of indication that it was indeed, a camping site. "Are you sure this is the camp site?" I continued, "Shouldn't there be a sign or something?" My team members started laughing. Frankie, one of the most resourceful and nature-educated people I had ever met, put up his finger and said, "You're right, hang on just a sec." I watched as he picked up a stick and started shoving it and moving it around in the dirt. Seconds later, he revealed his artwork. Outlined in the dirt, it said, "Campsite" with a little arrow drawn above pointing to the random spot in the woods. The others laughed again. "Very funny" I responded.

We started to set up camp as the night was almost halfway over. I laid out my cheap tarp and pulled out my 2-person tent. Before I unzipped the tent bag, I looked around at the others' sites. Everyone else had incredibly small 1-person tents and "bivy sacks," which are even smaller than a 1-person tent. I swear Frankie, the nature-loving one I mentioned earlier, just laid a tarp on the ground, hung a tarp above it by tying it to the trees, and said, "Okay boys, I'm all set." I gazed back down at my tent bag and hung my head low. "Well, I guess I'll have to use this one anyway." I pulled out the stakes and the rods, untucked the tent and the rain-fly, and started to set up camp.

After nearly 10 minutes, I had it all set up, and was ready to call it "home." Before I could turn around, one of the other members of my team named Troy shouted, "Nice mansion you got there! You having a party or what? If so, count me in." Frankie joined in, "Whoa man, is that one of those family tents?" Susan chuckled and chimed, "And I thought my 1-person tent was too big!" They were right. The label read '2-person, 3-season Tent,' but this thing was at least big enough to fit four average-sized people. Deciding to save face and give them some grief back, I simply replied, "Sounds like some of my teammates are a little jealous, eh? While you guys sleep in your prison cells tonight, I'll be having a nice stay in my luxury camp hotel." They looked at each other, smirked, and dropped the subject.

Sleeping was a challenge. I continued to roll over and over and couldn't get comfortable. Then, as if I was cursed, it started to rain. The pitter patter of the drops was worse than a leaking water faucet. It sounded like a tribe of annoying people tapping on my tent, purposefully trying to keep me awake. It was the first night in nearly six months that I was sleeping without my girlfriend next to me, and it proved to make things even more difficult. I was completely alone, completely out of my element, and completely uncomfortable.

I reassessed my situation. No pillow? No problem. Cleverly, I put a fresh pair of my boxers over my floppy water canteen and created a make-shift, head cushion. Cold and shaky? No problem! I just wrapped myself in my crappy sleeping bag and placed all of the clothes I had on top to add some weight. Then I pulled my beanie down completely over my face. No girlfriend? Again, no problem! I just tucked my oversized backpack into my sleeping bag with me and cuddled it as if it was her. Not quite the same, but all things considered, it was good enough. So that's how it went as the hours stretched on, and I continued to roll in and out of sleep.

As I woke to the sounds of birds chirping and the grunts of the others waking up, I realized that I must have only gotten about two hours of full sleep. My arms felt heavy, my legs felt beaten, and my whole body was sore and exhausted from the long hike the night before. I winced as I rubbed my feet, blistered with red spots and cuts all over. Reaching into my backpack (aka wilderness girlfriend), I pulled out a protein bar for breakfast. The flavor was Strawberry Vanilla, which sounded perfect for a nice morning meal. I crawled out of my tent, said good morning to the others, and noticed that each of them had a small camp stove. They heated up coffee and tea, and cooked eggs and oatmeal. I looked down at my protein bar, and despite the strawberry vanilla flavor I was just excited about, I immediately felt shorted. I knew I should have brought my grill! Jealous and still bitter about the comments they made the night before, I shouted, "If my tent is a mansion, then your grills are like restaurants!" They looked at me puzzled and I realized it wasn't a very good try. Troy peacefully replied, "I like my coffee, and I like my eggs, no other way to do it out here if you ask me." Susan agreed, "There's nothing like a warm meal on a cold morning."

I retreated to my tent, zipped myself inside, and miserably chewed on my protein bar.

"Alright everyone, let's go!" I crawled out of my tent as Eddie was making morning announcements, "I just got word on the radio that we are to leave our campsites in the next 10 minutes and make our way over to a new set of coordinates. Who knows what they have up their sleeves for this one, so bring everything with you except your tents. You can leave them set up. 10 minutes, not a second later. Let's go!" We all packed and got ready. I didn't bother changing my clothes, instead I figured a little deodorant would go a long way. I zipped up the tent, threw my backpack over my shoulders, and headed toward the others. Eddie prompted us on the coordinates, wrangled everyone together, and had us set off toward the first meeting location.

As we arrived, I knew we were in for a treat. The coordinates took us to the top of a giant, rock-faced cliff, where the bottom was about 50 feet below. The clouds up above were thunderous and flashing all over. Rain was pouring down and soaking everything. I gazed around and realized everyone was dressed in big, weather-proof jackets, which left me feeling a little

out of place with my little windbreaker. I learned a
very valuable lesson that day... water-resistant and
water-proof are two very different things. My jacket
was water-resistant, which basically meant that it
didn't do anything at all. It soaked all the way through,
and my shirt and skin were completely wet beneath. I
was really cold, completely wet, and terribly shaky.

Earl, the rescue commander, was waiting for us at
the cliff with lots of rope and some metal objects.
"Welcome to the rappelling station." Earl shouted.
"Here, you will have a chance to hook yourself up to
your own descender (rappel device), drop yourself
over the edge, and make your way to the ground. Then
you'll untie yourself, hike back up here on the trail
over there, and wait for next instructions." My heart
dropped. I had rock-climbed many times in the past,
but I always had a partner on a belay device, which
would guarantee my safety. I have never solo-climbed
with gear and I definitely have never rappelled alone.
This was a chance for me to really try something new.

Just as I wanted to back out, Eddie shouted, "Let's
make the new guy go first!" Susan joined, "Yeah, he
wanted to get a glimpse of what our lives were like...
he should go first!" Earl looked over at me, smiled, and

waved his hand for me to walk over. Lowering my eyes, I tried to nonverbally let Eddie and Susan know that I was not happy. I approached Earl and told him that I had never done this before. He laughed, assured me that I was safe, and started teaching me how to wrap the rope around the descender. A few moments later, I was harnessed in and ready to go. Earl yanked the rope that was attached to me and my body shifted forward. "Just checking," he laughed, then continued, "Okay, you're all set. Just walk over to the edge, turn around, and start making your way down. And make sure not to invert, okay?" Just as he said these words, thunder cracked loudly in the sky, and I jumped. Eddie called out, "Wait, Earl, are you sure he should be doing this? It looks like the lightning is heading our way. It's not exactly the safest place to be, hanging from a high cliff with a metal object, if you ask me." Earl looked to the others, looked at me, looked back at them, and cried out, "He'll be alright. We have at least a half hour or so before we're in any real danger." Still to this day, I'm not sure if they were messing with me or if I was actually unsafe.

"Okay Kev, you've got this," I thought to myself. I slowly walked toward the edge. "It just takes becoming comfortable with being uncomfortable, that's all." Each footstep moved slower as the nerves were firing off inside me. There I stood, at the edge of a cliff, 50 feet above the ground, with a single rope attached, without the slightest idea of what I was doing.

I turned around, nervously waved to the others, and started my descent. One of the first tips Earl gave me was to sit my butt low, to "lead with the butt," as he described. This should help me stay upright through the whole journey. So, I pretended like I was sitting in a chair and lowered my butt over the edge. Nice and slow, nice and easy. I was able to lower enough to move one of my feet from standing, to the side of the rock, horizontally.

The wet gloves I had on my hands made it difficult to get a good grip on the rope. Not to mention, my wet clothes made me twice as heavy and twice as miserable. I continued, hand over hand, letting a little rope go at a time to lower down slowly. Then, I was in trouble. As my second foot lifted off the ground, my other foot slipped on the wet rock. My soaked gloves let the rope slide through too quickly. I went free-falling. My whole body flipped over and dropped several feet before the rappelling device locked. I swung into the rock-face, banged my head and elbows, and dangled upside down.

I was literally hanging on by a thread. Panicked and trembling, I wrestled with the rope and different parts of the rock to try to flip myself back over. I heard the rescue members yell from above, "We told you not to invert!" "You better right yourself before something gives!" If only I knew how. So, I continued to wrestle and eventually, after what felt like forever, I was able to turn myself over and plant my boots back into the side of the cliff. My heart was pumping, my hands were shaking, and my mind was racing. "That's it!" They yelled, "Now just keep lowering down slowly." I screamed back, "I'm trying!"

One foot, then the next, then the next. Hand over hand. "Slowly, easily," I kept reminding myself. Just as I thought I was getting the hang of it, my boot slipped and I went upside down again, this time scraping my back and sliding down the rock about five feet before being jerked again by the rope and rappelling device. My breathing was rapid. My heart beat was revving like an oversized motor. Hanging there, I looked toward the ground and surprisingly, I laughed. Despite being close to death, and getting some serious cuts and bruises along the way, I was having one of the most extraordinary experiences of my entire life in one of the most unusual places I had ever been. Not only did I learn how to be self-sufficient in a remote setting and how to rappel over a cliff alone, but I also learned one of the most valuable life-lessons: that learning new things can make life better.

The sky cracked and boomed with thunder and lightning. My head pounded, my hands were shaky, and my body dangled. Sure, I was in pain, but it was masked with pure joy in that moment. I looked at the world upside down and fell in love with the whimsical view of the infinite blue ground and tree-filled sky. Like a pendulum in slow-motion, my body swayed back and forth. I dangled upside-down 50 feet above the ground, hanging on by a single thread, and I laughed. Then, I thought to myself, "This, right here, is where the magic happens."

The Science Behind Learning Something New

L earning new things can take us all over the world, help us meet new people, open up new doors, and even leave us upside-down on the edge of a very steep cliff in the wilderness. It can make us more powerful, more intelligent, more marketable, more interesting, more joyful, and more exciting. Learning new things has the power to drastically change our lives in a positive way. The best part is our brain will thank us for it, because the brain thrives when its learning.

According to scientists, nearly everything is learnable with the right mindset, energy, and guidance[1]. For those of us that have grown up thinking we're particularly bad at something, maybe it's a physical skill like basketball or ice-skating, or a mental skill like math or physics, it's completely possible to turn it around at nearly any age. Our ability to learn something new is actually helped or hindered by our mindset. When we think that we are capable and that we can get better, learn, change, and improve, we are adopting a *Growth Mindset*, which has been touted as one of the best approaches to learning[1].

Numerous studies have been done on this style of thinking, and it is becoming a staple in the education industry. Each semester, I'm invited to professional development workshops for various colleges and universities. One of the most common topics has been how to adopt a growth mindset, and how to help students believe they are capable of learning anything. The reason this style of thinking is so beneficial is that our brain has the ability to physically change over time, which is referred to as *Neuroplasticity*[1,2]. By actively changing the way we think over a period of time, our brain will change its default setting. Think of it like this. When we want to bulk up and build big muscles in our body, whether for looks or for function, we go to the gym each day and perform different work-outs. After some time, our muscles literally tear apart, repair themselves, and become physically bigger and stronger. The brain is pretty similar to this, although hopefully with a little less grunting and a little less bulge. When we engage in the learning process with a flexible and confident mindset each day, our brain becomes a little more powerful by firing new neural networks[1]. Ultimately, this strengthens our thinking muscles and helps us remember more information[3]. The good news is that we don't have to sign up at our local gym because learning takes place anywhere, anytime.

For our purposes, we are not talking about learning something in a professional setting. There is plenty of time for that in Elementary School, High School, and College. As a famous scientist puts it, "Our survival did not depend upon exposing ourselves to organized, pre-planned packets of information. Our survival depended upon chaotic, reactive information-gathering experiences"[4]. We don't really learn how to shoot an arrow by reading a textbook about archery. We learn by picking up a bow, pulling back the arrow, and firing. The same way that we can't learn to publicly speak or nail job interviews by just sitting around reading books. Instead, the only way to get better at being up in front of people, or sitting across from high-level professionals, is to actually put ourselves up in front of people and sit across from high-level professionals.

It's called *Experiential Learning*, or learning by doing. This style of learning has been touted by researchers over many years and across all disciplines[5]. In fact, many scientists believe that the process of making mistakes, reflecting, and continuing is one of the most favorable ways of learning[4,6]. In this way, there is no such thing as failure. Even if we are unable to become fluent in a new language or master a rhapsody on piano, in the great words of Randy Pausch, an inspiring and beloved professor at Carnegie Mellon University, "Experience is what you get when you didn't get what you wanted"[7]. Just like my experience with learning how to rappel off the side of a cliff, it took slipping and making huge mistakes in order to learn how to correctly place my boots in ways that would allow me to climb down safely. According to

John Medina, a professional brain consultant, "It is a scientific learning style we have explored literally for millions of years"[4]. In our ancestral days when our hair covered most of our body and we spoke in grunts, before Wikipedia and Google, there was no way to look up what would happen if we dropped a rock on our foot. If, however, we had the unfortunate experience of dropping one, we would immediately learn that dropped rock + foot = pain. Lesson learned. Life improved.

Perhaps one of the best parts about learning new things is that there is no right way or wrong way to go about it. There are infinite possibilities and strategies that can be customized, altered, shaped, and sized to fit every single individual on this planet (and probably even on other planets). As Benedict Carey writes in his book about learning, "...there are different strategies, each uniquely suited to capturing a particular type of information. A good hunter tailors the trap to the prey"[8]. It's up to us to try anything and everything to figure out our own best learning styles.

Another way to think about this is that we can do whatever we want to make the learning come to us. Tim Ferriss, a best-selling author and life-long accelerated learner, suggests that we learn by breaking down steps into four components that make up his 'secret sauce'[9]. Josh Waitzkin, another best-selling author, and also a world-champion at both chess and Tai Chi, suggests that the best way to learn is through themes, ideas, resilience, and performance psychology[10]. Are you starting to notice the differences? There are endless different ways to approach learning a new skill, and there is no one-size-fits-all method for everyone. For example, I love having instrumental music on in the background, yet my girlfriend enjoys having sitcoms on in the other room. My best friend likes absolute silence. So, the lesson here is don't get hung up on how to learn whatever it is that you learn next, but instead, focus on taking the first step and having fun along the way. As Ferriss says in a popular article, "To start something big, you have to first start something small"[11].

With access to so many resources, it has become possible to learn just about anything. For myself, I have created a list of all the things I hope to learn before I kick the bucket. Some of which are large-scale like learning a second language, becoming SCUBA certified, and trying out ice-climbing, while others are a bit smaller like attempting wake-surfing, driving a golf ball farther and straighter, and learning how to cook a perfectly seared salmon. The list is over 10 pages long and continues to grow each day. Along with many scientists, CEOs, and inventors, I believe that anything is possible, and that dreams are infinitely doable. It's all about having a growth mindset and adopting an attitude of believing in ourselves more than we ever did before. Now that you know learning new things can take you all over the world, can help you meet new people, make you more powerful, more marketable, and more incredible, the only question left to ask is: what will you learn next?

Comfort Challenge 10: Learn a Skill

One of the best ways to improve our quality of life and increase our value to the world is to learn new skills. We did it all the time as children: crawling, walking, running, talking, playing, singing, dancing, etc. Unfortunately, it is not something we do enough as we get older, which is exactly why it fits perfectly in this book.

For this challenge, you will be tackling something brand new in order to increase your skillset. Maybe you always wanted to discover a magic trick that you could show your friends, maybe you never learned how to ride a bike, or maybe there's a second or third language you've been thinking about adding to your repertoire. Now's the time! Go learn something new!

The Final Comfort Challenge

Congratulations! You are now ready for your final comfort challenge. Up to this point, you've had a chance to do some pretty amazing and wild things. From meeting strangers to spending time in nature, you have embarked on a path that few people have been brave enough to endure. Take a moment to congratulate yourself for making it this far!

The final comfort challenge is a little different than previous challenges. For this final challenge, you are invited to make a commitment to continue finding out what's possible in the world. Comfort challenges are all around us, in the form of cold showers, first dates, honest apologies, salary negotiations, spending a day without TV, wearing a top hat, riding a unicycle, and so on. While this might be the end of the book, it surely is just the beginning of a brand new, life-long adventure. The world is full of unfolded corners, uncharted territories, unprecedented opportunities, and infinite possibilities. Continue to explore, adventure, celebrate, sing, dance, and play along the way. Remember, comfort can always be found in the most unusual places...

And that, my friends, is **where the magic happens**.

Comfort Challenges

Baby
Steps

Act of
Kindness

Meet New
People

Say
Yes!

Mini-
Vacation

A Dose of
Nature

Be
Thankful

Adrenaline-
Rush

Fly
Solo

Learn a
Skill

Acknowledgements

This book is a dream come true, thanks to the help of many amazing people:

Tessa Daczyk, for all of her magnificence, for staying up late while I rambled about ideas, for spending beautiful summer days at the beach listening to me read chapters out loud, for reading the entire book several times, and for all of her amazing love.

Steve Rohr, who believed in this book when it was just a small idea during a Skype call, and helped bring it to life by publishing it! Thanks Steve!

Greg Godek, for being my book-mentor and spending hours with me at coffee-shops and Mexican food restaurants talking about how to make the book better.

Torrin DePierro, for being a true brother, a best friend, and for making so many of these wild stories possible.

Kerrya Corcoran, for being the coolest big sister a guy could ask for.

Sherry Corcoran, for being a loving mom, and for letting me explore, play in bands, and travel wherever I wanted when I was young.

Spencer Robbins, for believing in me more than I believed in myself, and for being a role model of positive, direct communication.

Erika Delemarre, for teaching me how to travel to new countries, and for letting me jump in freezing

Icelandic water, even though it was a bad idea from the start.

Michelle Francisco, for being a creative side-kick and for providing incredible illustrations (that unfortunately did not make it into the final edition).

Kyle Bowe, for helping me with the title and theme of the book, and for teaching me that losing your shit can be magical.

Andy Puddicombe, for introducing me to meditation and mindfulness, which has drastically improved how I live my everyday life.

Headspace, for being the single tool that has brought me presence, clarity, happiness, peace, and awareness.

My students, who have continuously supported and believed in me, and who have helped make my job the best in the world.

And a **HUGE** thank you to my **Secret Club of Advanced Readers**, who helped me with the final editing and formatting process: Isabelle Truong, Anaïs Barthelet, Jody Pham, Josie Pacheco, Shona Daily-Germino, Jorge Juarez, Shelby Ballo, Luke Henning, Jayden Lopez, Sara Popko, James Williams, Jeremea O. Songco, Matthew Snyder, Jennifer Ramirez, Paul Mansavage, Sean Freeny, Lissette Ontiveros, Sarah Mifflin, Sofia Long, Carly Donohue, Morgan Eide, Fiona Schmelzer, Marcela Diaz, Calah Beale, Camilo Cachán-Galvis, Juan Martinez-Rivera, Julio Munoz, and Josue Hernandez.

(I could not have finished the book without their help!)

References

The Science Behind Comfort Challenges

1. Adams, M., Bell, L. A., & Griffin, P. (2007).
    Teaching for diversity and social justice. New York:
    Routledge

2. Yerkes, R. M., & Dodson, J. D. (1908). The relation
    of strength of stimulus to rapidity of habit
    formation. Journal of Comparative Neurology and
    Psychology, 18, 459-482.

3. National Association of Cognitive-Behavioral
    Therapists. (2017). What is cognitive-behavioral
    therapy (CBT)? Retrieved from
    http://www.nacbt.org/whatiscbt-htm/

4. Byrne, R. W. (2013). Animal Curiosity. *Current
    Biology*, 23(11), 469-470.

5. Calhoun, A. J., Chalasani, S. H., & Sharpee, T. O.
    (2014). Maximally informative foraging by
    Caenorhabditis elegans. *eLife*, 3, e04220

6. Kidd, C., & Hayden, B. Y. (2015). The psychology
    and neuroscience of curiosity. *Neuron*, 88(3), 449-
    460.

7. Gruber, M. J., Gelman, B. D., & Ranganath, C. (2014). States of curiosity modulate hippocampus-dependent learning via the dopaminergic circuit. *Neuron*, 84, 486–496.

8. Engel, S. (2011). Children's need to know: curiosity in schools. *Harvard Education Review*, 81, 625–645.

9. Loewenstein, G. (1994). The psychology of curiosity: a review and reinterpretation. *Psychology Bulletin*, 116, 75–98.

10. Wayman, E. (2012). The earliest example of hominid fire. *Smithsonian*. Retrieved from http://www.smithsonianmag.com/science-nature/the-earliest-example-of-hominid-fire-171693652/

11. Prabhune, A. (2015). 10 Inventions that changed the world, but were made by mistake. *Storypick*. Retrieved from http://www.storypick.com/inventions-made-by-mistake/

12. NASA selects student's entry as new Mars rover name. (2011). *NASA*. Retrieved from https://www.nasa.gov/mission_pages/msl/msl-20090527.html

13. Ryan, R. M., & Deci, E. L. (2000). Self-determination theory and the facilitation of intrinsic motivation, social development, and well-being. *American Psychologist*, 55 (1), 68–78.

14. TEFD. (2017). Teaching for diversity, inclusion, and equity: The expanding comfort zone model. *The Institute for Teaching Excellence and Faculty Development*. Retrieved from https://www.umass.edu/ctfd/teaching/pdf/Expandi ng%20Comfort%20Zone%20Model.pdf

The Science Behind Acts of Kindness

1. http://www.visiticeland.com/DiscoverIceland/regio
    ns/highlands

2. BBC. (2015). Facebook's Mark Zuckerberg to give
    away 99% of shares. *BBC News*. Retrieved from
    http://www.bbc.com/news/world-us-canada-
    34978249

3. Kavanagh, J. (2016). Pirate of the care-ibbean:
    Johnny Depp dresses up as Captain Jack Sparrow
    to bring some festive cheer to sick kids at Great
    Ormond Street Hospital. *The Sun*. Retrieved from
    https://www.thesun.co.uk/tvandshowbiz/2370138/j
    ohnny-depp-dresses-up-as-captain-jack-sparrow-
    to-bring-some-festive-cheer-to-sick-kids-at-great-
    ormond-street-hospital/

4. Gridley, H. (2013). Jack Johnson donates 100% of
    tour profits to charity and promotes green touring
    initiatives. *Music for Good*. Retrieved from
    http://musicforgood.tv/2013/06/jack-johnson-
    donates-100-of-tour-profits-to-charity-promotes-
    green-touring-initiatives/

5. Parade. (2013). Celebrities' random acts of
    kindness. *Parade*. Retrieved from
    https://parade.com/67269/parade/random-act-
    niceness-10-celebrity/

6. The Huffington Post. (2013). Photograph of man teaching his girlfriend how to read the alphabet goes viral. *The Huffington Post: Good News*. Retrieved from http://www.huffingtonpost.com/2013/01/11/photograph-man-teaches-his-beloved-to-read-alphabet_n_2459389.html

7. Flam, L. (2012). The security guard who makes Disney dreams come true. *Today*. Retrieved from http://www.today.com/parents/security-guard-who-makes-disney-dreams-come-true-916096

8. Good News Network. (2014). Man acts as a human bench for elderly lady stuck on elevator. *Good News Network*. Retrieved from http://www.goodnewsnetwork.org/man-acts-as-human-bench-for-old-lady-stuck-on-elevator/

9. Winerman, L. (2005). The mind's mirror. *American Psychological Association*, 36(9), 48.

10. Keltner, D. (2009). Darwin's touch: Survival of the kindest. *Greater Good: The Science of a Meaningful Life*. Retrieved from http://greatergood.berkeley.edu/article/item/darwins_touch_survival_of_the_kindest

11. Darwin, C. (1871). *The Descent of Man* (Diversion Classics). New York: Diversion Books.

12. Szalavitz, M. (2012). How disasters bring out our kindness. *Time*. Retrieved from http://healthland.time.com/2012/10/31/how-disasters-bring-out-our-kindness/

13. Seppala, E. (2012). How the stress of disaster brings people together. *Scientific American*. Retrieved from https://www.scientificamerican.com/article/how-the-stress-of-disaster-brings-people-together

14. Buchanan, K. E., & Bardi, A. (2010). Acts of kindness and acts of novelty affect life satisfaction. *The Journal of Social Psychology*, 150(3), 235-237

15. Lyubomirsky, S., & Della Porta, M. (2008). Boosting happiness, buttressing resilience: Results from cognitive and behavioral interventions. In J. W. Reich, A. J. Zautra, & J. Hall (Eds.), Handbook of adult resilience: Concepts, methods, and applications. New York: Guilford Press.

16. Rand, D. G., Arbesman, S., & Christakis, N. A. (2011). Dynamic social networks promote cooperation in experiments with humans. *Proceedings of the National Academy of Sciences of the United States of America*, 108(48) 19193-19198.

17. Fox, G. R., Kaplan, J., Damasio, H., & Damasio, A. (2015). Neural correlates of gratitude. *Frontiers in Psychology*. Retrieved from http://journal.frontiersin.org

18. DiSalvo, D. (2009). Forget survival of the fittest: It is kindness that counts. *Scientific American*. Retrieved from https://www.scientificamerican.com/article/kindnes s-emotions-psychology/

19. Firozi, P. (2014). 378 people 'pay it forward' at Starbucks. *USA Today*. Retrieved from http://www.usatoday.com/story/news/nation-now/2014/08/21/378-people-pay-it-forward-at-fla-starbucks/14380109/

20. Fiedler, E. (2015). Philadelphia pizza lovers pay it forward one slice at a time. *NPR*. Retrieved from http://www.npr.org/sections/thesalt/2015/01/14/377 033772/philadelphia-pizza-lovers-pay-it-forward-one-slice-at-a-time

21. JetBlue. (2017). Flying it forward. *JetBlue*. Retrieved from http://jetblueflyingitforward.com/#!/intro

22. Pressman, S. D., Kraft, T. L., & Cross, M. P. (2014). It's good to do good and receive good. *The Journal of Positive Psychology*, 10(4), 293-302

23. Guerrero, L., Andersen, P. A., & Afifi, W. (2014). *Close Encounters: Communication in Relationships*. Los Angeles: Sage.

24. Cialdini, R. B. (1984). *Influence: The Psychology of Persuasion*. New York: HarperCollins.

25. Tsvetkova, M., & Macy, M. W. (2014). The social contagion of generosity. *Public Library of Science*. Retrieved from http://journals.plos.org/plosone/article?id=10.1371/journal.pone.0087275

26. Fowler, J. H. & Christakis, N. A. (2010). Cooperative behavior cascades in human social networks. *Proceedings of the National Academy of Sciences of the United States of America*, 107(12), 5334-5338.

27. Seppala, E. (2015). Why compassion is a better managerial tactic than toughness. *Harvard Business Review*. Retrieved from https://hbr.org/2015/05/why-compassion-is-a-better-managerial-tactic-than-toughness

28. AAT. (2014). Britain's workers value companionship and recognition over a big salary, a recent report revealed. *Association of Accounting Technicians*. Retrieved from https://www.aat.org.uk/about-aat/press-releases/britains-workers-value-companionship-recognition-over-big-salary

29. Wilkinson, A. (2015). In business, why kindness actually pays off. *Fortune*. Retrieved from http://fortune.com/2015/02/19/in-business-why-kindness-actually-pays-off/

30. Stanford University. (2017). Stanford bulletin: Explore courses. *Stanford University*. Retrieved from https://explorecourses.stanford.edu/search?view=catalog&filter-coursestatus-Active=on&page=0&catalog=&q=GSBGEN+524%3A+Compassion+and+Leadership&collapse

The Science Behind Meeting New People

1. Adler, R. B., Rodman, G., & Pre, A. D. (2014). *Understanding Human Communication* (12th edition). New York: Oxford University Press.

2. Vaillant, G. E. (2015). *Triumphs of Experience: The Men of the Harvard Grant Study*. Cambridge, MA: Harvard University Press.

3. Stark, K. (2016). Why you should talk to strangers. *TED*. Retrieved from https://www.ted.com/talks/kio_stark_why_you_should_talk_to_strangers/transcript?language=en

4. Boghani, P. (2017). Reducing solitary confinement, once cell at a time. *KPBS*. Retrieved from http://www.pbs.org/wgbh/frontline/article/reducing-solitary-confinement-one-cell-at-a-time/

5. Bond, M. (2014). How extreme isolation warps the mind. *BBC Future*. Retrieved from http://www.bbc.com/future/story/20140514-how-extreme-isolation-warps-minds

6. Maslow, A. H. (1943). A Theory of Human Motivation. *Psychological Review*, 50(4), 370-96.

7. Cook, G. (2013). Why we are wired to connect. *Scientific American*. Retrieved from https://www.scientificamerican.com/article/why-we-are-wired-to-connect/

8. Taflinger, R. F. (1996). Taking advantage: Social basis of human behavior. *Washington State University*. Retrieved from http://public.wsu.edu/~taflinge/socself.html

9. Adams, S. (2011). Networking is still the best way to find a job, survey says. *Forbes*. Retrieved from http://www.forbes.com/sites/susanadams/2011/06/07/networking-is-still-the-best-way-to-find-a-job-survey-says/#6499c6762754

10. Adler, L. (2013). The essential guide for hiring and getting hired: Performance-based hiring series. *Workbench Media*.

11. Glei, J. K. (n.d.) Why entrepreneurial thinking is for everyone now. *99U*. Retrieved from http://99u.com/articles/7161/why-entrepreneurial-thinking-is-for-everyone-now

12. Grant, A. M. (2014). *Give and take: Why helping others drives our success.* London: Penguin Books.

13. Edunov, S., Diuk, C., Filiz, I. O., Bhagat, S., & Burke, M. (2016). Three and a half degrees of separation. *Research at Facebook*. Retrieved from https://research.facebook.com/blog/three-and-a-half-degrees-of-separation/

14. RMIT Counseling Service. (2009). Developing self confidence, self esteem, and resilience. *Royal Melbourne Institute of Technology*. Retrieved from http://mams.rmit.edu.au/elh5d4nc7sfd.pdf

15. Garner, A. (1997). *Conversationally speaking: Tested new ways to increase your personal and social effectiveness*. New York: McGraw Hill.

The Science Behind Saying "Yes!"

1. Oxford University Press. (2016). How many words are there in the English language? Retrieved from https://en.oxforddictionaries.com/explore/how-many-words-are-there-in-the-english-language

2. Schwartz, T. (2015). The power of starting with 'Yes.' *The New York Times*. Retrieved from http://www.nytimes.com/2015/04/18/business/deal book/the-power-of-starting-with-yes.html?_r=0

3. https://www.facebook.com/BrianApplegateStatus

4. Bishop, R. (2016). Chaos. *The Stanford Encyclopedia of Philosophy*. Retrieved from http://plato.stanford.edu/entries/chaos/

5. Bussolari, C. J., & Goodall, J. A. (2009). Chaos theory as a model for life transitions counseling: Nonlinear dynamics and life's changes. *Journal of Counseling & Development*, 87, 98-107

6. Lorenz, E. N. (1993). *The essence of chaos*. University of Washington Press.

7. Skar, P. (2004). Chaos and self-organization: Emergent patterns at critical life transitions. *Journal of Analytical Psychology*, 49, 243–263.

8. Iafolla, T. (2017). The Key to Good Luck is an Open Mind. *Nautilus*. Retrieved from http://nautil.us//blog/the-key-to-good-luck-is-an-open-mind

9. Barrett, L. F. (2016). Are you in despair? That's good. *The New York Times*. Retrieved from https://www.nytimes.com/2016/06/05/opinion/sunday/are-you-in-despair-thats-good.html

10. Freeland, C. (2010). Google's culture of yes. *Reuters*. Retrieved from http://blogs.reuters.com/chrystia-freeland/2010/11/19/googles-culture-of-yes/

11. Solomon, M. (2015). Building a customer service culture of yes. *Forbes*. Retrieved from https://www.forbes.com/sites/micahsolomon/2015/03/16/the-answer-is-yes-now-what-was-the-question-building-a-customer-service-culture-of-yes/#258b8e123966

12. Our Insight. (2017). Creating a culture of 'yes.' *Ocean Prime*. Retrieved from https://www.ocean-prime.com/table-talk/view/articleid/212/creating-a-culture-of-yes

13. David, T. (2014). *Magic words: The science and secrets behind seven words that motivate, engage, and influence.* Prentice Hall Press: NY.

14. Merkin, R. S. (2006). Uncertainty avoidance and facework: A test of the Hofstede model. *International Journal of Intercultural Relations*, 30, 213-228

15. Baumeister, R. F., Bratslavsky, E., & Finkenauer, C. (2001). Bad is stronger than good. *Review of General Psychology*, 5(4), 323-370

The Science Behind Mini-Vacations

1. http://www.headspace.com

2. Chiesa, A., & Serretti, A. (2009). Mindfulness-based stress reduction for stress management in healthy people: A review and meta-analysis. *The Journal of Alternative and Complementary Medicine*, 15(5), 593-600.

3. Grossman, P., Niemann, L., Schmidt, S., & Walach, H. (2004). Mindfulness-based stress reduction and health benefits: A meta-analysis. *Journal of Psychosomatic Research*, 57(1), 35-43.

4. Kabat-Zinn, J. (2013). Full catastrophe living (revised edition): Using the wisdom of your body and mind to face stress, pain, and illness. New York, NY: Bantam Books.

5. Schure, M. B., Christopher, J., & Christopher, S. (2008). Mind-body medicine and the art of self-care: Teaching mindfulness to counseling students through yoga, meditation, and qigong. *Journal of Counseling & Development*, 86(1), 47-56.

6. Siegel, D. J. (2010). *Mindsight: The new science of personal transformation*. New York, NY: Bantam Books.

7. Mindfulness in the corporate world: How businesses are incorporating the eastern practice. (2012, August 29). *Huffington Post*. Retrieved from http://www.huffingtonpost.com/2012/08/29/mindfulness-businesses-corporate- employees-meditation_n_1840690.html

8. Wieczner, J. (2016). Meditation has become a billion-dollar business. *Fortune*. Retrieved from http://fortune.com/2016/03/12/meditation-mindfulness-apps/

9. Stanley, E. A., Schaldach, J. M., Kiyonaga, A., & Jha, A. P. (2011). Mindfulness-based mind fitness training: A case study of a high stress pre-deployment military cohort. *Cognitive and Behavioral Practice*, 18(4), 566-576.

10. Watson, J. (2013). Meditating marines: Military tries mindfulness to lower stress. *NBC News*. Retrieved from http://www.nbcnews.com/health/meditating-marines-military-tries-mindfulness-lower-stress-1B8050993

11. Gregoire, C. (2014). The brain-training secrets of Olympic athletes. *The Huffington Post*. Retrieved from http://www.huffingtonpost.com/2014/02/11/mind-hacks-from-olympic-a_n_4747755.html

12. Puff, R. (2014). How meditation won the super bowl. *Psychology Today*. Retrieved from https://www.psychologytoday.com/blog/meditation-modern-life/201402/how-meditation-won-the-super-bowl

13. Baer, R. A., Smith, G. T., Hopkins, J., Krietemeyer, J., & Toney, L. (2006). Using self- report assessment methods to explore facets of mindfulness. *Assessment*, 13(1), 27-45.

The Science Behind a Dose of Nature

1. Williams, F. (2015). This is your brain on nature. *National Geographic*. Retrieved from http://ngm.nationalgeographic.com/2016/01/call-to-wild-text

2. Nielsen, J. (2008). Americans spending less time in nature. *NPR*. Retrieved from http://www.npr.org/templates/story/story.php?storyId=18698731

3. Van Buren, A. (2016). 12 Secrets of New York's Central Park. *Smithsonian*. Retrieved from http://www.smithsonianmag.com/travel/12-secrets-new-yorks-central-park-180957937/

4. Central Park Conservancy. (n.d.). Park History. Retrieved from http://www.centralparknyc.org/visit/park-history.html?referrer=https://www.google.com/

5. http://www.visitphilly.com/outdoor-activities/philadelphia/fairmount-park/

6. http://www.laparks.org/griffithpark

7. http://www.cbsnews.com/news/presidio-san-francisco-unique-history-army-post-national-park-service-100-anniversary/

8. https://www.choosechicago.com/neighborhoods/north/lincoln-park/

9. https://www.balboapark.org/about/history

10. National Parks. (2016). Gardens in the sky. Skyrise Greenery. Retrieved from https://www.nparks.gov.sg/skyrisegreenery/

11. National Parks. (2015). City in a garden. Retrieved from https://www.nparks.gov.sg/about-us/city-in-a-garden

12. Wolf, K. L. (2002). Retail and urban nature: Creating a consumer habitat. *Nature and Retail Habitat*. Retrieved from http://plantsolutions.com/documents/CreatingAConsumerHabitat.pdf

13. Friedman, F. L., & Loria, K. (2016). 11 scientific reasons you should be spending more time in nature. *Business Insider*. Retrieved from http://www.businessinsider.com/scientific-benefits-of-nature-outdoors-2016-4/#1-improved-short-term-memory-1

14. Kahn Jr., P. H., Friedman, B, Gill, B., Hagman, J., Severson, R. L., Freier, N. G., Feldman, E. N., Carrere, Sybil., & Stolyar, A. (2008). A plasma display window? The shifting baseline problem in a technologically mediated natural world. *Journal of Environmental Psychology, 28*, 192-199.

15. Smith, L. (2014). Rx: 50mg nature. Slate. Retrieved from http://www.slate.com/articles/health_and_science/ medical_examiner/2014/07/doctors_prescribing_out doors_time_nature_is_good_for_you.html

16. Song, C., Ikei, H., Igarahsi, M. Takagaki, M., and Miyazaki, Y. (2015). Physiological and psychological effects of a walk in urban parks in fall. International *Journal of Environmental Research and Public Health, 12*, 14216-14228.

The Science Behind Being Thankful

1. Grant, A. M., et al. (2010). A little thanks goes a long way: Explaining why gratitude expressions motivate prosocial behavior. *Journal of Personality and Social Psychology*, 98(6), 946–55.

2. Lambert, N. M. et al. (2011). Expressing Gratitude to a Partner Leads to More Relationship Maintenance Behavior. *Emotion*, 11(1), 52–60.

3. Sansone, R. A. et al. (2010). Gratitude and Well Being: The Benefits of Appreciation. *Psychiatry*, 7(11), 18–22.

4. Seligman, M. E. P., et al. (2005). Empirical validation of interventions. *American Psychologist*, 60, 410–421.

5. Korb, A. (2012). The grateful brain: The neuroscience of giving thanks. *Psychology Today*. Retrieved from https://www.psychologytoday.com/blog/prefrontal -nudity/201211/the-grateful-brain

6. Fox, G. R., Kaplan, J., Damasio, H., & Damasio, A. (2015). Neural correlates of gratitude. *Frontiers in Psychology*. Retrieved from http://journal.frontiersin.org/article/10.3389/fpsyg.2 015.01491/full

7. UMass Dartmouth. (2017). The importance of gratitude. *University of Massachusetts Dartmouth.* Retrieved from http://www.umassd.edu/counseling/forparents/rec comendedreadings/theimportanceofgratitude/

8. Emmons, R.A., et al. (2003). Counting blessings versus burdens: An experimental investigation of gratitude and subjective well-being in daily life. *Journal of Personality and Social Psychology,* 84(2), 377–89.

9. Baker, D. & Kucher, K. (2011). Effects of power outage linger: Sewage spills, economic losses result from blackout. *The San Diego Union Tribune.* Retrieved from http://www.sandiegouniontribune.com/news/2011/sep/09/effect-of-power-outage-linger/

The Science Behind Adrenaline-Rushes

1. James, J. (2012). Animal instincts of the human body: A psychological and skeletal muscular analysis of adrenaline on the human body. *The People, Ideas, and Things Journal*. Retrieved from http://pitjournal.unc.edu/article/animal-instincts-human-body-psychological-and-skeletal-muscular-analysis-adrenaline-human

2. Csikszentmihalyi, M. (2004). Flow, the secret to happiness. *TED*. Retrieved from https://www.ted.com/talks/mihaly_csikszentmihalyi_on_flow

3. Dahl, M. (2016). You're excited, not nervous. You just keep telling yourself that. *Science of Us*. Retrieved from http://nymag.com/scienceofus/2016/03/youre-excited-not-nervous-you-just-keep-telling-yourself-that.html

4. Brooks, A. W. (2014). Get excited: Reappraising pre-performance anxiety as excitement. *Journal of Experimental Psychology*, 143(3), 1144-1158.

5. Dahl, M. (2015). What motivates extreme athletes to take huge risks? *Science of Us*. Retrieved from http://nymag.com/scienceofus/2015/05/what-motivates-extreme-athletes.html

6. Esposito, J. E. (2005). In the spotlight: Overcome your fear of public speaking and performing. *Bridgewater*, CT: In the Spotlight.

7. Kaufman, S. B. (2010). After the show: The many faces of the performer. *Psychology Today*. Retrieved from https://www.psychologytoday.com/blog/beautiful-minds/201008/after-the-show-the-many-faces-the-performer

8. Wise, J. (2010). The ultimate daredevil's guide to conquering fear. *Psychology Today*. Retrieved from https://www.psychologytoday.com/blog/extreme-fear/201006/the-ultimate-daredevils-guide-conquering-fear

9. MacKinnon, J. B. (2016). The strange brain of the world's greatest solo climber. *Nautilus*. Retrieved from http://nautil.us/issue/39/sport/the-strange-brain-of-the-worlds-greatest-solo-climber

10. Kashdan, T. B., & Silvia, P. J. (2008). Curiosity and interest: The benefits of thriving on novelty and challenge. *The Oxford Handbook of Positive Psychology*, 2, 367-375

11. Siegel, D. J. (2014). The ESSENCE of adolescence: Four important qualities of adolescence we can all cultivate. *Psychology Today*. Retrieved from https://www.psychologytoday.com/blog/inspire-rewire/201401/the-essence-adolescence

12. Zalocusky, K. A., Ramakrishnan, C., Lerner, T. N., Davidson, T. J., Knutson, B., & Deisseroth, K. (2016). Nucleus accumbens D2R cells signal prior outcomes and control risky decision-making. *Nature*, 531, 642-646.

13. Cummins, D. (2016). What Oprah and Warren Buffett can teach us about risk. *KPBS*. Retrieved from http://www.pbs.org/newshour/making-sense/what-oprah-and-warren-buffet-can-teach-us-about-risk/

14. Tierney, J. (2012). What's new? Exuberance for novelty has benefits. *The New York Times*. Retrieved from http://www.nytimes.com/2012/02/14/science/novelty-seeking-neophilia-can-be-a-predictor-of-well-being.html

15. Swink, D. F. (2010). Adrenaline Rushes: Can they help us deal with a real crisis? Harness the power of adrenaline. It can help you cope. *Psychology Today*. Retrieved from https://www.psychologytoday.com/blog/threat-management/201001/adrenaline-rushes-can-they-help-us-deal-real-crisis

The Science Behind Flying Solo

1. United States of America. (1964). Wilderness Act. Public Law 88-577.

2. Long, C. R., & Averill, J. R. (2003). Solitude: An exploration of benefits of being alone. *Journal for the Theory of Social Behaviour,* 33: 21–44.

3. Koch, P. (1994). *Solitude: A Philosophical Encounter.* Chicago: Open Court.

4. Guerrero, L., Andersen, P. A., & Afifi, W. (2014). *Close Encounters: Communication in Relationships.* Los Angeles: Sage

5. Bowlby, J. (1956). The growth of independence in the young child. *Royal Society of Health Journal,* 76, 587-591.

6. Dealing with Toddlers. (2017). *University of Illinois Extension.* Retrieved from https://extension.illinois.edu/toddlers/exploring.cfm

7. Janis, I. L. (1982). *Groupthink: Psychological Studies of Policy Decisions and Fiascoes. Second Edition.* New York: Houghton Mifflin.

8. Cain, S. (2012). The rise of the new groupthink. *The New York Times.* Retrieved from http://www.nytimes.com/2012/01/15/opinion/sunday/the-rise-of-the-new-groupthink.html

9. Suedfeld, P. (1982). *Aloneness as a healing experience. Loneliness: A sourcebook of current theory, research, and therapy.* New York: Wiley and Sons, pp. 54–67.

10. Harrison, A. A., Clearwater, Y. A., & McKay, C. P. (1991). *From Antarctica to Outer Space: Life in Isolation and Confinement.* New York: Springer Science & Business Media.

11. Wilson, T. D., Reinhard, D. A., Westgate, E. C., Gilbert, D. T., Ellerbeck, N., Hahn, C., Brown, C. L., & Shaked, A. (2014). Just think: The challenges of the disengaged mind. *Science,* 345(6192), 75-77.

12. Junger, S. (2016). *Tribe: On Homecoming and Belonging.* New York: Twelve.

The Science Behind Learning New Skills

1. Andreatta, B. (2014). The neuroscience of learning. *Lynda.com*. Retrieved from https://www.lynda.com/Higher-Education-tutorials/Neuroscience-Learning/188434-2.html

2. Bresciani-Ludvik, M. J. (2016). *The neuroscience of learning and development: Enhancing creativity, compassion, critical thinking, and peace in higher education.* Sterling, VA: Stylus Publishing.

3. Marcus, G. (2012). Happy new year: Pick up a new skill. *The New Yorker*. Retrieved from http://www.newyorker.com/news/news-desk/happy-new-year-pick-up-a-new-skill

4. Medina, J. (2008). *Brain rules: 12 principles for surviving and thriving at work, home, and school.* Seattle, WA: Pear Press.

5. Kolb, D. A., Boyatzis, R. E., & Mainemelis, C. (1999). Experiential learning theory: Previous research and new directions. *Department of Organizational Behavior, 1*, 1-38.

6. Goldman, B. (2011). Doctors make mistakes. Can we talk about that? *TED*. Retrieved from http://www.ted.com/talks/brian_goldman_doctors_make_mistakes_can_we_talk_about_that/transcript?language=en#t-333639

7. Pausch, R., & Zaslow, J. (2008). *The Last Lecture*. New York: Hyperion.

8. Carey, B. (2014). *How We Learn: The Surprising Truth About When, Where, and Why it Happens*. New York: Random House.

9. Ferriss, T. [The Next Web]. (2013, May 12). Tim Ferriss shares how to master any skill by deconstructing it. [Video File]. Retrieved from https://www.youtube.com/watch?v=DSq9uGs_z0E

10. Waitzkin, J. (2008). *The art of learning: An inner journey to optimal performance*. New York, NY: Free Press.

11. Ferriss, T. (2013). The ugly New York Times bestseller — The creative process in action. Four Hour Workweek. Retrieved from http://fourhourworkweek.com/2013/12/09/the-ugly-new-york-times-bestseller-the-creative-process-in-action/

CPSIA information can be obtained
at www.ICGtesting.com
Printed in the USA
FSHW04n1133040418
46545FS